THE FIRST

A Musical

Book by Joel Siegel
with Martin Charnin
Music by Bob Brush
Lyrics by Martin Charnin

S A M U E L   F R E N C H ,   I N C .
25 WEST 45TH STREET   NEW YORK 10036
7623 SUNSET BOULEVARD   HOLLYWOOD 90046
LONDON   *TORONTO*

PB922   466

Amateurs wishing to arrange for the production of THE FIRST must make application to SAMUEL FRENCH, INC., at 25 West 45th Street, New York, N. Y. 10036, giving the following particulars:

(1) The name of the town and theatre or hall in which it is proposed to give the production.
(2) The maximum seating capacity of the theatre or hall.
(3) Scale of ticket prices.
(4) The number of performances it is intended to give, and the dates thereof.
(5) The title, number of performances, gross receipts and amount of royalty and rental paid on your last musical performed.

Upon receipt of these particulars SAMUEL FRENCH, INC., will quote the amateur terms and availability.

Stock royalty and availability quoted on application to Samuel French, Inc.

For all other rights apply to Gottlieb, Schiff, Ticktin, Sternklar & Harris, P.C., Att: Richard Ticktin, Esq. 555 Fifth Avenue, New York, N.Y. 10017.

An orchestration consisting of a Piano Conductor which consists of Piano I, Piano II, Reed I, Reed II, Reed III, Reed IV, Reed V, Trumpets I, Trumpets II, Trumpets III, Trombone I, Trombone II, Trombone III, Horn, Cello, Bass, Guitar, Drums, and Percussion, will be loaned two months prior to the production ONLY on receipt of the royalty quoted for all performances, the rental fee and a refundable deposit. The deposit will be refunded on the safe return to SAMUEL FRENCH, INC. of all material loaned for the production.

Printed in U.S.A.

ISBN 0 573 68131 7

THE FIRST was presented by Zev Bufman and Neil Bogart, Michael Harvey and Peter Bobley at The Martin Beck Theatre in New York City on October 17, 1981. The settings were by David Chapman, the lighting was by Marc B. Weiss, the costumes were by Carrie Robbins and the sound was by Louis Shapiro. The musical director was Mark Hummel and the production stage manager was Peter Lawrence.

THE FIRST was directed by Martin Charnin and choreographed by Alan Johnson, with the following cast:

Patsy	BILL BUELL
Leo Durocher	TREY WILSON
Clyde Sukeforth	RAY GILL
Powers	SAM STONEBURNER
Photographer	THOMAS GRIFFITH
Branch Rickey	DAVID HUDDLESTON
Sorrentino	PAUL FORREST
Jackie Robinson	DAVID ALAN GRIER
Third Baseman	STEVEN BLAND
Junkyard Jones	LUTHER FONTAINE
Catcher	MICHAEL EDWARD-STEVENS
Rodney	RODNEY SAULSBERRY
Umpire	PAUL FORREST
Cool Minnie	CLENT BOWERS
Softball	PAUL COOK TARTT
Bucky	MICHAEL EDWARD-STEVENS
Equipment Manager	STEVEN BLAND
Redcap	MICHAEL EDWARD-STEVENS
Rachel Isum	LONETTE McKEE
Cuban Reporters	RODNEY SAULSBERRY STEVEN BLAND
Swanee Rivers	STEVEN BOOCKVOR
Casey Higgins	COURT MILLER
Hatrack Harris	D. PETER SAMUEL
Pee Wee Reese	BOB MORRISEY
Eddie Stanky	STEPHEN CRAIN
Dodger Coaches	JACK HALLETT BILL BUELL
Dodger Rookie	THOMAS GRIFFITH

```
Dodger Trainer ........................PAUL FORREST
Black Fans ........................BONCELLIA LEWIS
                                STEVEN BLAND
                     MICHAEL EDWARD-STEVENS
                                JANET HUBERT
                           RODNEY SAULSBERRY
Sheriff ..............................JACK HALLETT
Huey..................................JACK HALLETT
Brian Waterhouse ........................BILL BUELL
Opal ................................JANET HUBERT
Ruby ...........................BONCELLIA LEWIS
Mrs. Furillo .........................KIM CRISWELL
Mrs. Stanky......................MARGARET LAMEE
Red Barber...............................HIMSELF
Hilda Chester .........................KIM CRISWELL
Pittsburgh Catcher ..................THOMAS GRIFFITH
Hank Greenberg ......................STEPHEN CRAIN
```

SYNOPSIS OF SCENES
MUSICAL NUMBERS

ACT I

Scene 1: The Playing Field

Scene 2: Gallagher's Restaurant
JACK ROOSEVELT   Rickey, Durocher and
ROBINSON   Sukeforth

Scene 3: The Third Base Line
Comisky Park, Chicago
DANCIN' OFF THIRD   Jackie, Junkyard and
The Monarchs

Scene 4: The Locker Room of
The Kansas City Monarchs,
Comisky Park, Chicago
THE NATIONAL   Cool Minnie, Jackie, Junk-
PASTIME   yard and The Monarchs

Scene 5: Union Station, Chicago
WILL WE EVER KNOW
EACH OTHER   Jackie and Rachel

Scene 6: Branch Rickey's Office
THE FIRST   Jackie

Scene 7: The Havana Training
Camp of the Brooklyn
Dodgers
BLOAT   Durocher, Reporters and
the Dodgers

Scene 8: Outside a Ballpark,
Jacksonville, Florida
Reprise: THE FIRST   Jackie

Scene 9: The Locker Room
IT AIN'T GONNA WORK   Higgins and the Dodgers
THE BROOKLYN
DODGER STRIKE   Rickey and Durocher

Scene 10: Branch Rickey's Office
Reprise: JACK ROOSE-
VELT ROBINSON   Rickey
Reprise: THE FIRST   Rachel

Scene 11: The Playing Field

ACT II

The First

THE CURTAIN RISES *on a ball field, seen in silhouette. It is just before the game. The* PLAYERS, UMPIRES *and* COACHES *are milling around the field. There is an air of nervous anticipation about the moment.*
THEY *form a diagonal line, remove their caps and sing:*

ALL.
. . . O'ER THE LAND OF THE FREE
AND THE HOME OF THE BRAVE.

(*As* THEY *run to their respective field positions, we hear over the stadium p.a. system:*)

STADIUM ANNOUNCER. . . . would like to welcome you to this, the opening game of the 1947 National League season. (*Cheering.*) Ladeez and gentlemen . . . this is the starting line-up for the Brook-a-lyn Dod-juhs. (*Cheering.*) Batting lead-off, Numbah twelve, the second baseman, Eddie Stankeeeee. (*Cheering.* EDDIE STANKY *leaves a group of* PLAYERS *and runs to second base.*) Batting in the second po-sition, the short-stop, numbah one, Harold, "Pee Wee," Reeeeeese. (*Cheering.* PEE WEE REESE *leaves the group of* PLAYERS *and runs to short-stop.*) Batting in the third po-sition, the first baseman, numbah forty-two, Jack Roosevelt Robinson.

(*Suddenly, there is absolute silence. From the group of* PLAYERS, JACK ROBINSON *emerges.* HE *kneels, holding his bat, in the on-deck circle. As the lights begin to fade, we hear in voice-over:*)

RICKEY. Robinson, do you have the guts to play for the Brooklyn Dodgers?

RACHEL. Don't you understand, you're not going to be the first? There isn't going to be a first!

SUKEFORTH. Jack Robinson? Clyde Sukeforth. Branch Rickey wants to see you.

JACKIE. Rachel, listen. Clyde Sukeforth is a scout for the Brooklyn Dodgers. They came to me. No press, no tryout. They came to me. They came to me. (*This last phrase fades into an echo.*)

ACT ONE

SCENE 2

Gallagher's Restaurant on West 52nd Street, New York City. It is the Fall of 1946, immediately following the close of the regular National League season, in which the Brooklyn Dodgers have lost the pennant.

In the background is the famous meat locker and horseshoe-shaped bar. Downstage is a private table, surrounded by huge photographs of sports figures.

CLYDE SUKEFORTH, *a coach and scout for the Brooklyn Dodgers, and* LEO DUROCHER, *manager of the Dodgers, are at the table.* PATSY, *a waiter, is taking their order.*

SUKEFORTH. Patsy, did you save me an end cut of the prime rib?

PATSY. I'm sorry, Mr. Sukeforth, but they're all gone.

SUKEFORTH. How's the lobster today, Patsy?

PATSY. Not good, Mr. Sukeforth. They came in all green and funny. But I can recommend everything else on the menu. Would you like to order now?

LEO. Nah, we'd better wait for Mr. Rickey.

PATSY. Very well, Mr. Durocher. (PATSY *goes up to the bar to talk with the* REGULARS *gathered there.*)

LEO. So . . . go on. Go on.

SUKEFORTH. I spent four days tracking him down. Leo, he is the best prospect the Dodgers have ever scouted. Aggressive? A real holler guy! He can beat you from the bench. The only guy I've seen come even close is . . . Leo Durocher.

LEO. That good, huh?

SUKEFORTH. Leo, I've never seen anyone like him.

(JIMMY POWERS, *a particularly aggressive reporter, enters with a* PHOTOGRAPHER.)

POWERS. Leo! You know what I'm going to call you in tomorrow's column? "Manager of the Year." Managed to blow the pennant on the last out of the last inning of the last game of the season.

LEO. Hello, Mr. Powers.

POWERS. Good-bye, Mr. Durocher. When you gonna get fired, Leo? Before or after dessert?

SUKEFORTH. (*As if* POWERS *had told a joke.*) Fire Leo Durocher?

LEO. (*Laughing, but a little forced.*) That's the funniest thing I ever heard.

(SORRENTINO, *a busboy, enters with rolls and butter for the table.* HE *is barely civil to* DUROCHER.)

SORRENTINO. Nice to see you're able to show your face in public so soon, Mr. Durocher. (SORRENTINO *exits.*)

POWERS. Leo, is this the fourth year in a row you've lost the pennant? Or is this the fifth year in a row? (*Before Leo can answer,* BRANCH RICKEY, *the owner of the Brooklyn Dodgers, enters.* HE *is a big, expansive man with a great command of the English language.*) Mr. Rickey! (*To the* PHOTOGRAPHER.) Get this one. (RICKEY *poses with* DUROCHER *and* SUKEFORTH.) Good. I've always wanted a picture of The Last Supper.

RICKEY. (*Crossing down to* POWERS.) Mr. Powers, how nice to see you. If you will be in my office on Montague Street at 4:00 p.m. tomorrow afternoon, the Brooklyn Dodgers will officially announce that Leo Durocher . . .

POWERS. Is kaput.

RICKEY. . . . has been offered a new contract for the 1947 season.

POWERS. Some guys never learn. (POWERS *starts to exit with the* PHOTOGRAPHER, *but* LEO *stops him.*)

LEO. (*Confidentially.*) Mr. Powers. Try the lobster. (LEO *makes the "perfect" sign with* HIS *fingers.* POWERS *and the* PHOTOGRAPHER *exit.*)

RICKEY. (*Sitting down.*) Well, Sukey, did you see our prospect again?

SUKEFORTH. Yesterday in Cleveland. Mr. Rickey, he's all you hoped he was. And more.

RICKEY. (*Obviously excited.*) Judas Priest! Did you tell Leo?

SUKEFORTH. Yep. (*A pause.*) Almost everything.

LEO. (*To* RICKEY.) Almost everything? What'd he leave out?

RICKEY. Leo. I'm going to bring the first Negro ballplayer into the major leagues.

LEO. The first Negro . . . Oi vei! Mr. Rickey, you're out of your mind.

RICKEY. No, I'm not.

LEO. Who is this guy?

RICKEY. An infielder. A superior athlete. Fiercely intelligent. During the war, an officer in the United States Cavalry.

LEO. Can he run?

RICKEY. He looks awkward. He's pigeon-toed. His elbows flay, his hips sway, his shoulders rock, as if he's about to take off in seven separate directions all at once.

LEO. (*Exasperated.*) Sukey! Can he run?

(*MUSIC.*)

JACK ROOSEVELT ROBINSON

SUKEFORTH.
ELECTRIFYING
BASE-RUNNER SECOND TO NONE
THE ART OF FLYING
IS
JACK ROOSEVELT ROBINSON

LEO. (*Spoken.*) Jackie Robinson. Yeah. Plays short-stop with the Kansas City Monarchs. Weird stance at the plate, though. Can he hit?

RICKEY.
FEROCIOUS LINE DRIVES
LIKE BULLETS
SPRAYED FROM A GUN
YOU'LL LIKE THOSE FINE DRIVES

RICKEY and SUKEFORTH.
BY JACK ROOSEVELT ROBINSON!

RICKEY.
YES, IT'S A RISK

BUT A RISK WORTH TAKING
JUDAS PRIEST
I HAVE FOUND ME MY MAN.
    SUKEFORTH.
NO ONE IN BASEBALL
MAKES WAVES THE WAY
THAT OUR LEADER CAN.
    LEO. (*Spoken.*) A colored guy in the major leagues.
    RICKEY. (*Spoken.*) Leo, what do six to five, four to three and one to nothing mean to you?
    LEO.
TWELVE GAMES LAST SEASON
TWELVE GAMES WE LOSE BY A RUN
    RICKEY.
BUT WE COULD CHANGE THAT
WITH
JACK ROOSEVELT ROBINSON!
    ALL.
PLAYERS NEED SPIRIT
AND STYLE AND COLOR
    RICKEY.
I'M CONVINCED THAT HE'S
JUST SUCH A LAD.
    LEO.
LEAVE IT TO RICKEY.
TO FIND US A COLOR
WE'VE NEVER HAD.
    RICKEY. (*Spoken.*) Come on. Let's eat.
    LEO. (*Spoken.*) When are we gonna take a look at him?
    RICKEY. (*Spoken. To* SUKEFORTH.) They have any more games scheduled?
    SUKEFORTH. (*Spoken.*) They're playing in Chicago tomorrow.
    RICKEY. (*Spoken.*) Sukey, if you take a plane you can be in Chicago in six hours. Go and bring Robinson back with you.
    LEO.
YOU SLY OLD CODGER
YOU'LL MAKE YOUR BUMS
NUMBER ONE
    ALL.
OUR LATEST DODGER IS
    RICKEY.
JACK ROOSEVELT

SUKEFORTH and LEO.
JACK ROOSEVELT
ALL.
JACK ROOSEVELT
ROBINSON!

ACT ONE

SCENE 3

*Comisky Park, Chicago. The Kansas City Monarchs are playing
the Chicago American Giants.*
*It is the ninth inning, with the Kansas City Monarchs at bat. The
following action is entirely choreographic:*

(*MUSIC: DANCIN' OFF THIRD.*)
(*A bat crack is heard, and* JACKIE ROBINSON *comes streaking
around the bases, stopping at third base. The third baseman
and* JACKIE *eye each other, warily.* JUNKYARD JONES, *the
pitcher, returns to the mound.* JACKIE *dances off third, trying to rattle the pitcher.* JUNKYARD *shakes off several signs
from his* CATCHER, *all the while watching* JACKIE. JACKIE
takes a long lead-off, JUNKYARD *checks* HIM, *forcing*
JACKIE *back to third.* JUNKYARD *takes a long wind-up and
pitches, but* no ball leaves HIS *hand.* JACKIE *races for home,
slides, and is tagged out by the* CATCHER, *who miraculously
has produced a ball.*)

UMPIRE. OUT!
JACKIE. (*Leaping to his feet, in a rage.*) Out!? Are you a blind
man? He never threw the ball. (*The* UMPIRE *begins to walk
slowly off the field, paying no attention to* JACKIE.) The pitcher
has got to pitch the God-damned ball! And he never threw it! He
never threw the ball.
UMPIRE. (*Never breaking stride.*) I said, "Out," Robinson.
This ball game is over.
JACKIE. You are a blind man. Don't forget your cup.
ANOTHER PLAYER. (*Shouting after the* UMPIRE.) You are
dumb!
JACKIE. (*Shouting to* JUNKYARD.) Junkyard! You didn't pitch
that ball, did you?

JUNKYARD. It's no disgrace to have been snookered by Junkyard Jones. That, Robinson, is an honor.

JACKIE. (*Going after* HIM.) You honor me like that one more time . . .

(COOL MINNIE, *seeing a potential fight, comes across the field and pulls* JACKIE *into the locker room, away from an aggravatingly smug* JUNKYARD JONES.)

ACT ONE

SCENE 4

The Locker Room of the Kansas City Monarchs at Comisky Park, Chicago, immediately following the previous scene.

COOL MINNIE. (*Pulling* JACKIE *into the locker room.*) Ahh, we get him next time.

JACKIE. Next time? I'm the tieing run. I had him this time.

COOL MINNIE. Aw, you young yet. We all been juked and jived by Junkyard Jones.

SOFTBALL. The man speaks the truth, Jackie.

COOL MINNIE. Anyway, that's what the fans come to see.

JACKIE. I come to win.

COOL MINNIE. Go take your shower, Jack. We're going to The Pump Room to see Nat King Cole.

JACKIE. How are you guys going to get into The Pump Room?

SOFTBALL. Same way we got in last time.

(RODNEY *puts a towel, wrapped like a turban, around* COOL MINNIE's *head.*)

RODNEY. Table for twelve for the Maha Raja.

SOFTBALL. (*Acting like a very impressed lackey.*) Right this way, sir. Right this way.

JACKIE. Thanks, Cool Minnie, but Rachel's coming in from California. I've got to pick her up at the station.

(CLYDE SUKEFORTH *enters the locker room. Unsure of just which player is* JACKIE, HE *goes to* SOFTBALL *for help.*)

SOFTBALL. (*Amused.*) Hey, Jack. You got a visitor.

SUKEFORTH. (*Crossing to* JACKIE *and extending* HIS *hand.*) Jack Robinson? I'm Clyde Sukeforth. God, I had a devil of a time finding you. Today, you're number 8. Last week in Memphis, you were number 19, and yesterday in Cleveland, 31.

JACKIE. (*Curious, but wary.*) In this league, you wear whatever's clean. Can I . . .

(BUCKY *enters from the shower, singing at the tops of his lungs.*)

BUCKY.
CHICAGO, CHICAGO
THAT TODDLIN' TOWN . . .

SOFTBALL. Sing it, Bucky!

RODNEY. Shut up, Bucky!

JACKIE. Can I do something for you?

SUKEFORTH. I work for the Brooklyn Dodger organization. I'm here at the personal request of Mr. Branch Rickey, the President of the Brooklyn Dodgers. Mr. Rickey would like to see you in New York, tomorrow.

(*Some of the* MONARCHS *have begun to eavesdrop.* JACKIE *strolls up to* HIS *locker.*)

JACKIE. Tomorrow? Oh. What for?

SUKEFORTH. Well, he'll have to tell you that himself. (*Noticing all the* MONARCHS *staring at* HIM *suspiciously.*) But . . . uh . . . I can assure you that Mr. Rickey's intentions are quite honorable.

(COOL MINNIE *signals to* JACKIE *to come over to* HIM. HE *whispers to* JACKIE *as if this were a secret of great importance.*)

COOL MINNIE. Jackie! You gonna get married.

(*The* MONARCHS *all laugh.* SUKEFORTH *is beginning to get uncomfortable.*)

BUCKY. (*Singing.*)
HERE COMES THE BRIDE
HERE COMES THE BRIDE . . .

SOFTBALL. Shut up, Bucky!

RODNEY. Sing the song, Bucky!

JACKIE. Look, Mr. Sukeforth, I don't mean to give you a hard time, but you can tell your Mr. Rickey that he's a little bit late.

EQUIPMENT MANAGER. (*Entering with a towel cart.*) Hey.

SUKEFORTH. You mean you're signed with another club?

EQUIPMENT MANAGER. (*Louder, since no one paid attention to* HIM *the first time.*) Hey!

(*The* MONARCHS *all cross to the cart and throw in* THEIR *towels and uniforms.*)

JACKIE. No, I mean I've been there. Twice. Once when the White Sox came through Los Angeles. Jimmy Dykes, the manager, I think he wanted to sign me, but the front office wouldn't let him.

(JUNKYARD JONES *enters the locker room.* JACKIE *spots* HIM *and crosses angrily in front of* HIM.)

JACKIE. Junkyard, that wasn't baseball out there. That was vaudeville.

JUNKYARD. Robinson, don't bite the hand that feeds you. (*Seeing* SUKEFORTH.) Sukey! Is that you?

SUKEFORTH. (*Going to* JUNKYARD *and shaking* HIS *hand warmly.*) Sure is, Junkyard. I haven't seen you since we played winter ball in Panama. How've you been?

JUNKYARD. Reasonable. Reasonable. Still throwin' . . . junk. (JUNKYARD *tosses* HIS *towel into the cart after an elaborate wind-up.*)

SUKEFORTH. I know. I was watching you today.

JUNKYARD. And yourself?

SUKEFORTH. Having a little trouble convincing Mr. Robinson here that Mr. Branch Rickey really does want to see him.

JUNKYARD. (*Impressed.*) True?

SUKEFORTH. True.

(*All eyes turn to* JACKIE, *who stands at* HIS *locker, facing away from* THEM. *Suddenly,* HE *turns angrily to* SUKEFORTH.)

JACKIE. Do you know who Isadore Muchnick is? Some Boston politician. Got up and made a big, fat speech one afternoon, threatened to close the ballparks on Sunday—Boston being such a religious town—if they didn't give the nice colored boys a chance. So, they brought me up to Fenway Park to catch a few flies and field a few grounders. And when I got up to bat, I must've hit a hundred balls off that damn left field wall. And then the Red Sox personnel director's *assistant* hands me a yellow card to fill out, doesn't say anything, doesn't even call me "Robinson," just says, "We'll get back to you." (JACKIE *turns away from* SUKEFORTH *and sits on a bench. There is a moment of very uncomfortable silence, which is broken by* BUCKY *singing:*)

BUCKY. (*Singing.*)
OH, BOSTON, BOSTON
THAT TODDLIN' TOWN . . .

SUKEFORTH. (*Crossing to* JACKIE.) Mr. Rickey knows about Boston. This is different.

COOL MINNIE. Man, this ain't different! The N-double-A-C-P been picketing Yankee Stadium.

BUCKY. Mayor LaGuardia starts some committee. Some New York councilman makes a speech. We read it. We *can* read, you know.

COOL MINNIE. Some of us can. (*Referring to* SOFTBALL.) He can't. I told him about the speech. (SOFTBALL, *playing the game, assumes an appropriately uneducated expression.*) So, your Mr. Rickey needs a *boy* to get the heat off him.

RODNEY. We heard it all before.

COOL MINNIE. We heard it so many times, we know it by heart.

(*MUSIC.*)

THE NATIONAL PASTIME

COOL MINNIE.
IT'S TIME
THAT WE INTEGRATE
THE NATIONAL PASTIME!

MONARCHS.
NATIONAL PASTIME!

JUNKYARD. (*Speaking.*) Oh, Lordy, is it that time *again*? Hmmm, Hmmm, Hmmm!

COOL MINNIE.
AND IT CAN'T BE
A FEEBLE TRYOUT
LIKE THE LAST TIME!

MONARCHS.
LIKE THE LAST TIME!
JUNKYARD. (*Speaking.*) 'Dat time, I say 'dat time was a fiasco!
With the accent on . . . asco!
COOL MINNIE.
THERE'S NOTHING BUT
WHITE MEN
PLAYING IN THE LINE-UP
THAT'S NINE-OUTA-NINE UP
SO, YOU'VE GOTTA SIGN UP
   COOL MINNIE. (*Speaking.*) Someone!
   EQUIPMENT MANAGER. (*Speaking.*) Someone black!
   COOL MINNIE. (*Speaking.*) Or brown!
   SOFTBALL. (*Speaking.*) Or tan!
   BUCKY. (*Speaking.*) Or even a mulatto!
   ALL.
AND WE'LL SING
THE OBLIGATO! (*Pause.*)
   ALL.
SHA-DOOBIE-DOO
DOOBIE-DOO
DOOBIE-DOO
DOOBIE-DOO-WA

SHA-DOOBIE-DOO
DOOBIE-DOO
DOOBIE-DOO
DOOBIE-DOO-WA
   COOL MINNIE.
WHO CAN FIELD?
WHO CAN SLIDE?
WHO MAKES PITCHERS TERRIFIED?
WHO WE GLAD IS ON OUR SIDE?
   ALL.
THIS YEAR'S NIGGER!
   COOL MINNIE.
WHO BRINGS LIFE
TO THE GAME?
EV'RYBODY KNOWS HIS NAME!
AT WHOSE HEAD DO THEY TAKE AIM?
   ALL.
THIS YEAR'S NIGGER!

Cool Minnie.
WELCOME TO THE MAJORS
Rodney.
YOU ARE GONNA FLOWER
Softball.
LET'S GO SPLIT A RHEINGOLD!
Junkyard.
RACE YOU TO THE SHOWER!
Cool Minnie.
WELCOME TO THE MAJORS
YOU THE CUTEST MONKEY!
Bucky.
LET'S GO DOUBLE DATING
Cool Minnie.
LET ME BE!
Equipment Manager.
NO! LET ME BE!
All.
NO! LET ME BE
HIS BUNKIE!

WHO BATS CLEAN-UP
NUMBER FOUR
CLEAN-UP BATTER
AND MUCH MORE
Cool Minnie and Monarchs.
CLEANS THE WINDOWS
Jackie and Monarchs.
AND THE FLOOR
All.
THIS YEAR'S NIGGER!
Sukeforth. (*Speaking.*) Robinson! I think Mr. Rickey deserves to be heard, too.
Monarchs. (*Speaking.*) Right!
Cool Minnie. (*Speaking.*) And you know what Mr. Rickey's gonna say?
All.
GOOD FIELD
GOOD HIT
GOOD LORD
GOOD NIGHT!
Cool Minnie.
WHAT A FANCY FIELDER

HIT IT
AND HE'LL KETCH IT
  BUCKY. (*Pointing to* SOFTBALL.)
SAY, DON'T I KNOW YOUR BROTHER?
  BLAND.
AIN'T HE STEPPIN FETCHIT?
  SOFTBALL. (*Speaking.*) Yassir, that be him.
  COOL MINNIE.
RAISE HIS YEARLY SALARY
DOUBLE IT, BY GOLLAH!
OH, MY GOODNESS GRACIOUS!
  EQUIPMENT MANAGER.
THAT MAKE TWENTY—
  JUNKYARD.
NO, THAT MAKE THIRTY—
  SOFTBALL.
NO, THAT MAKE FIFTY DOLLAH!
  ALL.
HERE HE COMES
CLEAR THE TRACK
BIG AS LIFE
BIG AND BLACK!
  COOL MINNIE.
OHHHHHHHHH,
MR. RICKEY
THIS HERE BE JACK!
HE'S THIS YEAR'S
NIGGER
NIGGER
  ALL.
NIGGER
UNH!
UNH!
UNH!
UNH!
UNH!

(*The number ends with all the* MONARCHS *surrounding a very
    uncomfortable* SUKEFORTH. *Again,* BUCKY *breaks the
    tension.*)

  BUCKY. (*Singing.*)
OH, BROOKLYN, BROOKLYN
THAT TODDLIN' TOWN

(*All the* MONARCHS *return to* THEIR *lockers, leaving* JACKIE *and* SUKEFORTH *alone.*)

SUKEFORTH. Robinson, Mr. Rickey has been scouting dozens of colored ballplayers. And you're the one he wants to see.

JACKIE. You know, it all feels like old Junkyard's hesitation pitch. Where he winds up and stops. And then he winds up some more and stops again. But he never does let go of the damn ball.

SUKEFORTH. Well, maybe. But wouldn't it be a shame if when we finally decided to throw it, you didn't have anyone up at bat? It's your decision. The Broadway Limited leaves Union Station at 7:15 tonight. Mr. Rickey hopes you're on it. I do, too. (*To the* MONARCHS.) Gentlemen. (HE *leaves.*)

ACT ONE

SCENE 5

A platform at Union Station in Chicago.
A train has just arrived, discharging passengers. A REDCAP *enters with a luggage cart. One of the passengers with* HIM *is* RACHEL ISUM.

TRAIN ANNOUNCER. (*Voice Over.*) The City of New Orleans is now boarding passengers at Gate Four. All abooooooard! The Broadway Limited to Pittsburgh, Philadelphia, and Pennsylvania Station, New York City, is now accepting passengers at Gate Ten. Gate Ten, the Broadway Limited.

(*All the* PASSENGERS *have now left the platform, leaving* RACHEL *alone with the* REDCAP.)

REDCAP. You sure I can't help you, Ma'am?

RACHEL. Thank you, but I'm sure he's on his way.

REDCAP. He's a fool if he ain't.

(*The* REDCAP *exits.* RACHEL *is alone for a few moments on the platform.* JACKIE *rushes onto the platform, out of breath and carrying a suitcase. He greets* RACHEL *with a huge, loving embrace and many kisses.*)

JACKIE. Oh, Rachel, Rachel. It is good to see you. It's been a long time.

RACHEL. Too long.

JACKIE. You're even prettier than I remembered.

RACHEL. Oh, Jack.

JACKIE. And I remembered absolutely beautiful.

(THEY *separate.* JACKIE *assumes that* RACHEL *knows about* HIS *meeting with* SUKEFORTH *and the trip to New York.*)

JACKIE. Well?

RACHEL. (*Having no idea what* HE'*s talking about.*) Well?

JACKIE. Clyde Sukeforth didn't meet you here to tell you I'd be late?

RACHEL. (*Crossing to the luggage cart.*) Who? No. I thought . . . extra innings or something.

JACKIE. Oh. (*Crossing to* RACHEL.) Rae, listen. Branch Rickey, the President of the Brooklyn Dodgers, wants to see me in New York . . .

RACHEL. Right away.

JACKIE. Tomorrow.

RACHEL. What did he say? What do they want to see you about?

JACKIE. (*Sitting beside* RACHEL *on the cart.*) I've got this feeling in my gut that this might be the real thing.

RACHEL. Did he say that?

JACKIE. No. But do you know who the Brooklyn Dodgers *are*?

RACHEL. Yes. And I know who the Chicago White Sox are. And the Boston Red Sox.

JACKIE. Rae, this is different. They came to *me.* They've been scouting *me.* Listen to this. No press. No tryout. They want to talk to *me.* It's different this time. I know it is.

RACHEL. How many white major league teams are there? Sixteen? Do all sixteen of them have to disappoint you and use you and hurt you before you understand that you're not going to be the first. That nobody's going to be the first. That there isn't going to be a first.

JACKIE. It's different this time.

RACHEL. (*Taking* JACKIE'*s hand and holding it in front of* HIS *face.*) Oh, Jack. *This* is what's different.

(*A train has arrived, and the platform is filled with* PASSENGERS.)

JACKIE. Rae, please. I'm not a doctor, I'm not a lawyer, I don't run a business and I can't sell insurance. It's going to sound prideful, but I really believe that God picked me for this. He's got to have given me this talent for a reason. Rae . . . I've got to go. But I'll be back on Monday. We'll be able to . . .

RACHEL. We're never together. Do you know when we were the closest? (JACKIE *shakes* HIS *head, "No."*) When you were in the Army, and I was in nursing school.

JACKIE. But we were a thousand miles apart.

RACHEL. And you wrote every day.

JACKIE. I still write. I'll write you from Brooklyn.

RACHEL. Then you wrote letters. Now you mail me clippings. "Robinson pounds three hits against Indianapolis Clowns." Do you think I love you because you can pound three hits against the Indianapolis Clowns? Monte Irvin got four hits against the Homestead Greys. Should I love Monte Irvin more than I love you?

JACKIE. (*Smiling.*) You wouldn't even like Monte Irvin. He's halfway bald, he's got this pointy little nose . . .

RACHEL. Jackie . . .

TRAIN ANNOUNCER. (*Voice Over.*) The Broadway Limited, making stops in Pittsburgh, Harrisburg, Philadelphia, Trenton, Newark and Pennsylvania Station, New York City, is now ready to accept passengers at Gate 10. All abooooard!

JACKIE. (*Impulsively.*) Babe, come to Brooklyn with me. We'll get married in Brooklyn.

RACHEL. (*After a pause.*) *Babe*? We'll get married in California, *Babe*, at my Mother's house, after we spend enough time together to discover whether or not we should even *get* married!

JACKIE. Rachel, you're so fussy!

(*MUSIC.*)

WILL WE NEVER KNOW EACH OTHER

RACHEL.
WILL WE EVER
KNOW EACH OTHER

WELL ENOUGH?
GET TO GROW
AND GET TO SHOW
AND TELL ENOUGH?
THERE ARE A THOUSAND THINGS
THAT PLEASE YOU
THERE ARE A THOUSAND MORE
THAT THROW YOU
BABE—
I DAMN WELL
BETTER KNOW YOU BETTER
THAN I KNOW YOU!

JACKIE. (*Spoken.*) Know me better?

YOU KNOW ME—
NO DRINKING . . .
NO SMOKING . . .

(*Spoken.*) And I'm gorgeous!

YOU KNOW ME—
YOUR HERO
WE'D MAKE
TERRIFIC BABIES!
YOU'LL LOVE THE WAKING UP
BESIDE ME
YOU'LL LOVE THE WAY
I "VELVET GLOVE" YOU

BOTH. .
BABE

RACHEL.
I DAMN WELL
BETTER LIKE YOU BETTER
THAN I LOVE YOU!

JACKIE. (*Spoken.*) Rachel Isum, you like me. Like it or not, you like me. You like my one crummy blue suit, and you like that I send you clippings from the road. And you *love* that I've got this dream!

BOTH.
WE MAY NEVER
KNOW EACH OTHER
WELL ENOUGH

THERE MAY NEVER
BE THE TIME
TO TELL ENOUGH
 RACHEL.
BUT WE HAVE GOT TO
START OUT SOMEWHERE
 JACKIE.
NO NEED TO START
THE NEEDING OF YOU
 BOTH.
BABE!

(THEY *embrace. The shrill blast of a train whistle reminds* JACKIE
 that the Broadway Limited is about to leave. HE *looks at*
 RACHEL, *torn, and then runs to the gate.* RACHEL *turns sadly
 away, and notices that* JACKIE *has forgotten* HIS *suitcase.*)

 RACHEL. Jack! (HE *returns and* SHE *hands* HIM *the suitcase.*)
If your meeting with Mr. Rickey makes the papers, send me the
clipping.

(JACKIE *smiles, kisses* HER, *and runs for the train.*)

HOW COULD I LOVE YOU
ANY BETTER
THAN I LOVE YOU.

(SHE *picks up* HER *suitcases and slowly leaves the platform.*)

ACT ONE

SCENE 6

BRANCH RICKEY's *Office on Montague Street in Brooklyn.*
*Although the room is sparely furnished, it is cluttered with vari-
 ous sports awards and trophies. On the rear wall hangs a
 huge photograph of the 1946 Brooklyn Dodgers Baseball
 Club.*
BRANCH RICKEY *is seated at* HIS *desk studying a folder of papers. The inter-com buzzes.*

 RICKEY. (*Into the inter-com.*) Yes, Jane.

JANE. (*Over the inter-com.*) Mr. Sukeforth and Mr. Robinson are here to see you.

RICKEY. Send them in, Jane. Send them in.

(SUKEFORTH *enters with* JACKIE *and crosses to the desk.*)

SUKEFORTH. Mr. Rickey, this is Jack Robinson.

RICKEY. (*Offering* HIS *hand.*) Mr. Robinson. Branch Rickey. Thank you, Sukey. Thank you very much.

(SUKEFORTH *leaves.* RICKEY *shows* JACKIE *to a seat beside the desk.*)

RICKEY. How was the trip?

JACKIE. Fine. Long.

RICKEY. (*Appraising* JACKIE. *Not really hearing* HIM.) Good. Good. (*A pause.*) What a lovely tie.

JACKIE. Thank you.

RICKEY. I see you prefer the four-in-hand. I, of course, am wedded to the old-fashioned bow. Not that sartorial splendor is one of my virtues. In fact, one of our writers—Holmes of The Eagle—once asked me where I go to get my suits trampled. (THEY *chuckle nervously.*) But I don't imagine you thought I asked you to travel to New York to discuss haberdashery.

JACKIE. I hope not.

RICKEY. And my efforts at casual conversation have not eased your anxieties as to just why I have asked you here.

JACKIE. Not really, Mr. Rickey.

RICKEY. Well, then, Robinson, let's get right down to cases. Do you have a girl?

JACKIE. I beg your pardon?

RICKEY. Do you have a girl?

JACKIE. I was expecting something more along the lines of . . . how do you do against right-handed pitching.

RICKEY. I know how you do against right-handed pitching. I don't know if you have a girl. And it is important. (JACKIE *nods, "Yes."*) Good. When we finish here today, you'll want to call her. You'll need her by your side. Robinson, this is your scouting report. But it's more than that. I know about your youth, your college days—UCLA's first four-letter man. I know about your military career. (JACKIE *becomes visibly uncomfortable.*) I understand. I read this, and I understand. If you were white, the noun would be "leader," and the adjective "competitive." But you are black, so the noun is "trouble-maker," and the adjective is "uppity." I want you to know that I admire everything this report tells me. And it tells me everything—except the one thing only you can tell me. Do you have the guts to play for the Brooklyn Dodgers of the National Baseball League?

JACKIE. (*Quickly.*) Yes, I do.

RICKEY. Do not be confused by desire, son. You will not be just another athlete coming into the National League. Oh, I wish it were that simple—a question of hits, runs and errors, the information they carry in a box score. A baseball box score is a wonderfully democratic thing. It does not divulge a player's size, or his religion, or his color, or his politics.

JACKIE. All it tells is how he plays the game. And that's all that counts!

RICKEY. All that *should* count.

JACKIE. Mr. Rickey, all I want is to be treated fairly.

RICKEY. Judas Priest, son, you will *not* be treated fairly. (HE *crosses to* JACKIE.) You will be cursed. Your color will be cursed. Your family will be cursed. That vicious epithet, "nigger," will seem a veritable compliment. And if you are to break the color line and play in the major leagues, you must accept it all and accept it silently.

JACKIE. Mr. Rickey, are you looking for a black man who's afraid to fight back?

RICKEY. I'm looking for a ballplayer with guts enough *not* to fight back. For to fight, Robinson, is to lose. We are no army, we have few allies. The other owners? They will deny it, after the meeting they burnt their records in shame, but the vote was 15 to 1 against having Negroes in organized baseball. The players? 60% of all major-league ballplayers were born in the South. Perfect fodder for the bigots and hate-mongers who want to see you fail. And you cannot fail.

JACKIE. Mr. Rickey, do you realize what you're asking me to do?

RICKEY. Oh, yes. Do you? Robinson, we're in a ballgame. I'm on the opposing team, and I've been on you all day long. Sambo! Shine! Jigaboo! Junglebunny! And you've heard me—all day long. You're at short-stop, I'm on first. There's a slow grounder to second base—a double-play ball for sure. You cover the bag, get the throw, and I come in sliding—my spikes high. The umpire shouts, "Out!" and I jump up and all I see is your big, black face. "How do you like that, nigger boy!" I say. And I take a swing at your cheek. What do you do, Robinson? What do you do?

(JACKIE*'s fists are clenched. After a moment,* HE *relaxes.*)

JACKIE. Mr. Rickey . . . I've got two cheeks.

RICKEY. (*Looking at* JACKIE *admiringly.*) It won't be forever. One year. One silent season. I know it's not a perfect plan, but at the moment it's the only one we have.

JACKIE. My brother, Mack? My brother is a college graduate. He won a silver medal in the '36 Olympics. Only Jesse Owens beat him. Do you know what Mack does, Mr. Rickey? He's a street cleaner. I can take the pain. I've been taking it all my life.

SUKEFORTH. (*Entering in a mild panic.*) Mr. Rickey. Mr. Rickey. I'm sorry, but there must be fifteen reporters outside. And I don't know what to tell them.

RICKEY. (*Rising and crossing to the door.*) Wait for me, Robinson. Like General MacArthur, I shall return. (HE *exits with* SUKEFORTH. JACKIE *takes in the room, really seeing it for the first time. Finally,* HIS *eyes land on the team photo.*)

(*MUSIC.*)

THE FIRST

JACKIE.
TOO MANY TIMES
I'VE BEEN BOUNCED AROUND.
TOO MANY BUBBLES BURST.
TOO MANY YEARS
PRAYING THERE WOULD BE
A FIRST.

DAY AFTER DAY
I KEEP WONDERING—
HAVE I BEEN BLESSED
OR CURSED?
RACHEL IS RIGHT
THERE MAY NEVER BE
A FIRST.
BUT MY WHOLE LIFE
HAS BEEN AIMED AT THIS MOMENT

GOD KNOWS IF IT EVER COMES AGAIN
AND THE MOMENT BELONGS
JUST AS MUCH TO ME—
AS IT DOES
TO THE BROTHERHOOD OF MEN.

"JACKIE, THAT'S THE WHITE MAN'S TREE."
"JACKIE, THAT AIN'T RIGHT TO DO."
MOMMA, I CAN CLIMB!—
"JACKIE, AIN'T THE TIME
FOR YOU."
"JACKIE, THAT'S THE WHITE MAN'S POOL.
COLOREDS SWIM WHEN HE GETS THROUGH."
MOMMA, I CAN RACE!—
"JACKIE, AIN'T THE PLACE
FOR YOU."

SO MANY TIMES I'VE BEEN BOUNCED AROUND
SO MANY BUBBLES BURST
IT ISN'T CRAZY TO WANNA BE
WHAT I HAVE TO BE
WHAT I'M GONNA BE!
"JACKIE, THAT'S THE WHITE MAN'S GAME,
NOW YOU WANT TO PLAY IT, TOO?"
MOMMA, I CAN CLIMB!
MAYBE IT'S THE TIME!
MOMMA, I CAN RACE!
MAYBE, IT'S THE PLACE!
MOMMA, I CAN PLAY!
"JACKIE, IT'S A DAY
FOR YOU."

(JACKIE *ends the song as* HE *began it—looking at the team photo.* RICKEY *enters and pauses for a moment, just watching* JACKIE.)

RICKEY. It seems the press has gotten wind of this little assignation. The onslaught is at hand. What do we tell them?

JACKIE. You haven't said anything about a contract.

RICKEY. Spring training begins February 20 in Havana. You will train with us there at our expense. Then, when you sign with the Brooklyn Dodgers, a three thousand dollar bonus, six hundred dollars a month, and I'll buy you out of whatever time remains in your Kansas City Monarch contract.

JACKIE. Mr. Rickey, why are you doing this?

RICKEY. (*Quietly.*) Baseball. The great *American* game. The *National* pastime. Do you hear the stress I put on those words—national? American? But what color is the ball, and the bases, and the uniforms, and the players in those uniforms? It is time to change that. (*Shifting tone slightly.*) There is another reason. It is as venal and as opportunistic as picking up a ten dollar bill off a sidewalk. I run a ballclub. It's a good ballclub. I would like to make it a great ballclub. And, Robinson, you are the most electrifying ballplayer in the United States of America.

(JACKIE *extends* HIS *hand*. RICKEY *takes it.* THEY *shake hands, sealing* THEIR *bargain, and walk out of the room.*)

ACT ONE

SCENE 7

The Brooklyn Dodger Training Camp in Havana, Cuba. It is February, 1947, at the beginning of Spring training.
LEO DUROCHER *is on the field talking with* JIMMY POWERS *and two* CUBAN REPORTERS.

LEO. . . . now, this is the third decade of my baseball career, and I'll tell you something. In all that time, I never had a boss call me upstairs and congratulate me for losing like a gentleman. (*The* REPORTERS *mumble and write.*) "How you play the game," is for college boys. When you play for money, winning is the only thing that matters. (*The* REPORTERS *mumble and write.*) You show me a good loser in professional sports . . .

LEO and POWERS. . . . and I'll show you an idiot.

CUBAN REPORTER. Que dice?

LEO. Loco in the cabeza.

POWERS. Leo, do you feel good about training down here in Cuba?

LEO. Yeah. Three weeks here. Three weeks playin' our way through the South on our way to Brooklyn. Yeah, I'd rather start training here in Havana than in thumb-up-your-nose Florida.

POWERS. Sure you would. No casinos in Florida. You're gonna have to be a good boy, Leo.

LEO. Mr. Powers, this was Mr. Rickey's idea. You ask him. I know about two things. I know about baseball, and I know about winning. Now, somebody once said I'd run over my own mother if it'd help me win the pennant, and when she saw that, it brought tears to that poor, old woman's eyes. But I'll tell you this: if dear, sweet mom doesn't learn to hit the curve-ball by April the first, she ain't gonna make the team. Now, the 1947 Brooklyn Dodgers are a sleek, stream-lined, well-oiled, machine. (*The* DODGERS *straggle onto the field. Some are smoking, all are over-weight and out of shape, with prominent beer bellies.*) They're a team of tough, hard, hungry young athletes. When better ballplayers are built, Brooklyn'll build 'em.

(*The* REPORTERS *are writing furiously in* THEIR *notebooks about the condition of the* DODGERS. LEO *signals for the* DODGERS *to begin exercises.* HE *turns to explain to the* REPORTERS.)

(*MUSIC.*)

BLOAT

LEO.
BLOAT,
BLOAT,
BLOAT.
IT'S MERELY
BLOAT,
BLOAT,
BLOAT.
IT'S THE YEARLY
BLOAT,
BLOAT,
BLOAT.
IT GOES AWAY.

BEER,
BEER,
BEER.
IT'S WINTER
BEER,

BEER,
BEER.
THEY GET IN T'
BEER,
BEER,
BEER.
WHAT MORE TO SAY.
   REPORTERS.
THIGHS
THERE'S A LOT OF THIGHS
OF ENORMOUS
SIZE . . .
   LEO.
BUT ON OPENING DAY
(*To the* DODGERS.)
HEY!
THEY'LL BE THIN
   DODGERS. (*Beginning to exercise faster and harder.*)
AS RAILS!
   LEO.
THEY'LL BE HARD
   DODGERS.
AS NAILS!
   LEO.
THEY WON'T BREAK THE SCALES
AND SHOULD THEY THIRST
   DODGERS.
AND SHOULD WE THIRST.
   LEO. (*Spoken.*) OK, let's work it out now.
   DODGERS.
IT'S APPLE JUICE
AND H-2-O
   LEO.
'CAUSE EVEN BRAINLESS
DUMBBELLS KNOW
THAT FAT
   LEO and DODGERS.
FAT, FAT, FAT, FAT.
DON'T FINISH FIRST.
   LEO. (*Spoken to the* REPORTERS.) Fellows, I want you to come over here and meet some of the players. This is Hatrack Harris, one of our catchers. And this is Pee Wee Reese.

POWERS. Leo, we all know Hatrack Harris and Pee Wee Reese. What about the "noble experiment?"

LEO. What "noble experiment," Mr. Powers?

POWERS. C'mon, Leo. What about this Jackie Robinson business?

LEO. Jackie Robinson?

POWERS. Jackie Robinson.

LEO	DODGERS
NOW, AS FAR AS	BLOAT
THE SIGNING OF ROBINSON GOES,	BLOAT
IT MAY WORK,	BLOAT
IT MAY NOT,	IT'S
BUT AS EVERYONE KNOWS,	MERELY
THIS ENTIRE AFFAIR	BLOAT
HAS BEEN HANDLED WITH CARE	BLOAT
BY BRANCH RICKEY.	BLOAT
	IT'S
	MY
AND FROM WHAT	YEARLY
I'VE BEEN TOLD	BLOAT
BY THE SCOUTING REPORT,	BLOAT
HE'S A HELLUVA FIELDER	BLOAT
(AT SECOND OR SHORT)	IT
BUT HE JUST DOESN'T	GOES
WALK ON THIS TEAM!	A-
IT'S A LITTLE MORE TRICKY.	WAY.
I GOT STANKY	BEER
AND ROJEK—	BEER
YOU KNOW I GOT REESE—	BEER
AND FOR ME	IT'S
REESE HAS GOT	WINTER
AN UNBREAKABLE LEASE,	BEER
SO IF THIS FELLA ROBINSON WORKS,	BEER
IT'S AT ONE OF THE BASES.	BEER
	WE
IF HE HITS	GET
LIKE A HAMMER	IN T'
(THE WAY THAT THEY SAY)	BEER
IF HE RUNS	BEER
LIKE A DEER,	BEER

THEN WE GIVE HIM AN "A",	WHAT
AND THE TRUTH IS	MORE
I COULDN'T CARE LESS	TO
WHAT THE COLOR HIS FACE IS	SAY.

POWERS. (*Spoken.*) And the Cardinals?

LEO	DODGERS
NOW, THE CARDS	THIGHS
ARE AS TOUGH	
AS A COBBLESTONE STREET!	THERE'S
IF WE'RE GONNA CONTEND	
THEN WE GOTTA COMPETE!	A LOT OF
AND THAT STARTS ON DAY ONE	
OF SPRING TRAINING—	THIGHS
(WHEN WEEKS SEEM TO FLY BY)	
	OF
AND I PROMISE YOU THIS—	
(IF YOU HAD ANY DOUBT)	E-NOR-
ON THE DODGERS	
IT'S SHAPE UP, MY FRIEND,	MOUS
OR SHIP OUT!	
SO THE BLUBBER	SIZE
THAT'S HERE IN HAVANA	
HAD BETTER GO BYE-BYE!!	

(*The* DODGERS *are now exercising rapidly and with perfect precision. And, as* LEO *predicted,* THEY *are all "thin as rails," and "hard as nails."*)

DODGERS.
HEY!
WE WON'T LOSE
  LEO.
OH, NO!
  DODGERS.
NO LEADS!
WE'LL BE SLIM
  LEO.
AS WHAT?
  DODGERS.
AS REEDS!
WE'LL GO OFF OUR FEEDS
BEFORE WE BURST!

LEO.
BEFORE WE BURST!
  DODGERS.
THE TEAM THAT SCORES—
THE TEAM THAT WINS—
IS THE TEAM THAT HAS
NO DOUBLE CHINS!
'CAUSE FAT
  LEO.
FAT, FAT, FAT, FAT.
  DODGERS.
DON'T FINISH
(ONE, TWO, THREE, FOUR, FIVE, SIX, SEVEN, EIGHT,
NINE, TEN, ELEVEN, TWELVE.)
  LEO and DODGERS.
FIRST!

(*As the unison exercise breaks up, the* DODGERS *begin to practice
  individually. Some checking* THEIR *batting swings, some
  playing catch, some checking equipment.* CASEY HIGGINS, *a
  pitcher, goes to an isolated corner of the field.* HE *is followed there by* POWERS.)

POWERS. Higgins! Higgins, is it true? $17,000?
CASEY. I told Mr. Rickey fifteen game winners don't camp
cheap. $18,000.
POWERS. How's the fast ball?
CASEY. Straight and hard.
POWERS. And the curve?
CASEY. Straight and hard.
POWERS. Tell me the truth. How do you boys feel about this
Jackie Robinson?
CASEY. Don't make no never-mind to me, long as he ain't on
the team. Rickey must have two hundred boys down here tryin'
out for the Dodgers.

(LEO, *who is with the* CUBAN REPORTERS, *notices* POWERS *talking with* CASEY. HE *walks quickly to* THEM *to break up the
  conversation.*)

LEO. All right, Higgins, let's get to work. Mr. Powers, right
this way, please.
POWERS. Thanks a lot, Casey.

(HATRACK HARRIS, *in* HIS *catcher's equipment, sidles over to* CASEY.)

HATRACK. Casey.

CASEY. What?

HATRACK. I was shagging flies with this kid outfielder, Snider? Edwin Snider? Trying to get names for our petition.

CASEY. And?

HATRACK. I said, "Hey, Edwin, what y'all think of this Jackie Robinson boy?"

CASEY. And what'd he say?

HATRACK. He said — you ain't gonna believe this. First his eyes got big as jelly doughnuts, and he got gooey all over, like he's got Dorothy Lamour waitin' for him under the bleachers.

CASEY. C'mon, Hatrack, c'mon!

HATRACK. And he says that he just can't wait to meet him! He says when he was a little boy in California, this Robinson was an All-American football star, and one time li'l Edwin waited half-an-hour for his autograph!

CASEY. Least ole Rickey could've done was get us some ordinary nigger.

HATRACK. Where is the nightfighter, anyway?

CASEY. I was down at the office yesterday, makin' some time with that chesty li'l switchboard girl, when she put through this important call from *Mistah* Robinson.

SUKEFORTH. (*Crossing to* HATRACK *and* CASEY.) Gentlemen. What's it going to be — baseball or bullshit?

HATRACK. Sukey. (HATRACK *and* CASEY *make a show of getting to work.*)

CASEY. (*Under* HIS *breath.*) Bullshit. Well, it seems they threw him offa this airplane when it landed in New Orleans. And then they threw him off'n another one in Pensacola. So, he regretted to report, he'd be a tiny bit late gettin' here to Havana, seein' as how him and his new wife cain't find no plane to fly no nigras! (THEY *laugh.*) How many names we got?

HATRACK. Five or six. Swanee's got the paper. (*Shouts.*) Hey, Swanee. (SWANEE *stops batting practice and jogs over to* CASEY *and* HATRACK.)

HATRACK. (*Conspiratorially.*) Swanee, you got it?

SWANEE. I don't know if I got it, the Doc says it'll take two weeks to know for sure.

CASEY. C'mon, Rivers. You got the paper?

SWANEE. Sure I got the paper. (SWANEE *reaches under* HIS

jersey and produces a folded piece of paper. All three men look around to make sure no one is watching.)

CASEY. (*Checking the paper.*) Pee Wee ain't on here.

SWANEE. I ain't talked to Pee Wee.

HATRACK. (*Shouting to* PEE WEE.) Hey! Reese! (PEE WEE *stops playing catch and jogs over.*)

CASEY. Hey, Pee Wee, where you from?

PEE WEE. Kentucky. Ekron.

CASEY. Ekron? Sounds like something you take when your stomach gets sour.

PEE WEE. It's a nice town.

CASEY. (*Placatingly.*) I know. I know. I mean I've never been there, but I'm sure it's a nice town. Little square in the middle. Town Hall over there, Baptist Church over there. (CASEY *gestures right, then left.*)

PEE WEE. No. Baptist Church over there. Town Hall over here. (PEE WEE *gestures left, then right.*)

HATRACK. And bang in the middle of that little square, there's a big, ole granite statue of Johnny Reb, right?

PEE WEE. Right.

SWANEE. Lots of names carved into that granite, I'll bet. Boys who fought in that war of secession.

PEE WEE. Lots.

CASEY. Well, we got a way you can do something for the memory of those boys who fought so valiantly! (CASEY *hands the paper to* PEE WEE.)

PEE WEE. (*Reading.*) "We, the undersigned members of the Brooklyn Dodgers Baseball Club, respectfully refuse to play ball with the Negro . . ." (*Looking up at* CASEY.) You know, we lost that war. And you guys are going to lose this one. And maybe your jobs.

CASEY. Our jobs? This Robinson ain't after *our* jobs. He plays short-stop, Colonel, same as you.

SWANEE. Maybe better.

CASEY. Well, Colonel, what are you going to do about it?

PEE WEE. There's only one way he's going to play short-stop for the Brooklyn Dodgers. He's going to have to win that job. From me. And he won't win it, because I'm the best damn short-stop in the National League.

HATRACK. (*Horrified.*) You mean you're going to let this nigger use our locker room, and our showers, and our towels, and stay in our . . .

(PEE WEE *shoves the petition back into* CASEY's *glove, pushes through the group and returns to practice.*)

CASEY. He's as bad as that Jewboy, Branca.

SWANEE. Branca's Catholic.

CASEY. They're the worst kind. Hell, we don't need him. The way I figure it, we got five, six names already.

SWANEE. Six.

CASEY. We got at least half the team on our side. Maybe they ain't signing, but they're thinking. And when that big, black buck shows his big, black face . . .

(SWANEE *nudges* CASEY *and points to another part of the field.* JACKIE *has come hesitantly onto the field and is trying to join a "pepper" game in progress.* JACKIE *is ignored by the* PLAYERS. JACKIE *then walks over to* CASEY, HATRACK *and* SWANEE. HE *nods to* THEM. CASEY, *over-polite, tips* HIS *hat and smiles. These three then start their own "pepper" game, pointedly refusing to throw the ball to* JACKIE. THEY *circle* JACKIE, *throwing the ball over* HIS *head and around* HIM. JACKIE *shakes* HIS *head in disgust, and starts to walk to another part of the field. Suddenly, a loose ball hits* JACKIE *on the back.* HE *turns angrily, thinking the hit was deliberate.* PEE WEE *runs after the loose ball, picks it up and starts to leave. But as* HE *looks from* CASEY *to* JACKIE, HE *understands the situation.* PEE WEE, *after a moment, tosses the ball to* JACKIE. JACKIE *tosses it back, underhand to* PEE WEE. THEY *continue to toss the ball underhand, backing further and further from each other. Then,* THEY *begin to throw over-hand, and the only sound on the field is the "thwack" of the ball in* THEIR *two mitts.*)

ACT ONE

SCENE 8

The Player's Entrance to a ballpark in Jacksonville, Florida. In the background is an empty grandstand. A high, chain-link fence separates the playing field from the outside of the ballpark.

SWANEE *is hitting fungoes, which other* DODGERS, *including* JACKIE, *are fielding. A number of black fans are pressing against the fence to get a glimpse of* JACKIE.
A local SHERIFF *enters, crosses to the gate in the fence and goes onto the field.*

SHERIFF. Any of you boys knows who's in charge here?
SWANEE. Is there a problem, Sheriff?
SHERIFF. Not yet.

(SWANEE *points to* SUKEFORTH. *The* SHERIFF *goes over to* SUKE-FORTH, THEY *have a conversation, and* SUKEFORTH *exits. A group of black fans enters, and stand outside the gate.*)

EARL. That's him. That's him. Mr. Robinson! Mr. Robinson! (JACKIE *comes over to the fence.* EARL *shoves a piece of paper and a pencil through the fence.*) Could you, please? To Earl, Junior. He's just six and every afternoon he makes me bring home the newspaper just so he can read about Jack Robinson.
RACHEL. (*Entering and waving to* JACKIE.) Jack.
JACKIE. Rachel!

(*The* FANS *congregate around* RACHEL.)

EARL. Mrs. Robinson, I saw your husband play short-stop for the Kansas City Monarchs. He's gonna make a fine short-stop for the Dodgers.
RACHEL. He's not playing short-stop. Yesterday, they moved him to first base.
EARL. (*Not missing a beat.*) He's gonna be a fine first baseman for the Dodgers.

(*The* SHERIFF *comes out of the gate, followed by an angry* LEO.)

LEO. What do you mean, no game?
SHERIFF. No game.
LEO. What's wrong?
SHERIFF. Equipment failure.
LEO. The dirt's broken? The grass don't work?
SHERIFF. Uh, uh. The lights.
LEO. It's eleven o'clock in the morning. We play the Detroit Tigers at one. Are you expecting an eclipse?

SHERIFF. (*Walking away, not listening.*) No game.

LEO. You pea-brained son-of-a-bitch! I got a major league season starting in three weeks. How the hell am I supposed to get this team ready for it? Over a card-table?

(SUKEFORTH *walks to* LEO *and puts a hand on* HIS *arm to calm* LEO *down.* LEO *angrily shakes* SUKEFORTH *off. The* SHERIFF *walks slowly back to* LEO.)

SHERIFF. (*Quiet and deadly.*) We do not raise our voices in Duval County. And I strenuously advise you to lower yours. And quietly, but quickly, move on. (HE *walks away, near the* BLACK FANS.) Oh, and don't forget to take your colored mascot with you. (HE *exits.* EVERYONE *looks at* LEO *for a decision. After a moment,* HE *signals to* SUKEFORTH *to pack up the team.*)

CASEY. (*Mock-sympathetic.*) That's OK, Leo, we'll lead the League in pinochle.

(*The* DODGERS *take* THEIR *equipment and leave.* JACKIE *comes through the gate and crosses to* RACHEL.)

LEO. Jack . . . I don't think you should leave Rachel alone. Stay here. We'll bring the bus around.

JACKIE. (*To* LEO.) Thanks. (*To* RACHEL.) Are you all right?

RACHEL. I'm a little scared, but I'm all right.

BLACK FAN. I knew they'd never let no colored man play no baseball in Jacksonville, Florida.

RACHEL. Not today, but it is going to happen.

BLACK FAN. Lady, you don't look like you're asleep, but you sure is dreaming. Gonna happen, gonna happen, gonna happen. If I could put "gonna happen" in my bank account, I'd be the richest man in Jacksonville.

BLACK WOMAN. How long you staying in Florida?

RACHEL. We leave tomorrow.

BLACK WOMAN. For New York City?

JACKIE. For Georgia.

BLACK WOMAN. (*Turning and leaving.*) Lord have mercy!

BLACK FAN. Mr. Baseball Player. You fast? (JACKIE *nods,* "*Yes.*") Good thing you fast. (*Turning to other* FANS.) C'mon, let's get outta here.

ANOTHER BLACK FAN. I think we'd better wait till they get on the bus, huh? (*The* FANS *separate to wait for the bus.*)

JACKIE. (*To* RACHEL.) It's not much of a honeymoon, is it Rae?

RACHEL. Jack, we said, "For better or worse." We're just starting off on the wrong half, that's all.

JACKIE. Rae . . .

RACHEL. I'm fine.

JACKIE. But, Rae, the better is here, too.

(*MUSIC.*)

THE FIRST (Reprise)

JACKIE.
THIS TIME
A DREAM
DIDN'T FALL APART!
THIS TIME
NO BUBBLE BURST!
THOUGH IT WAS SO
FULL OF FEAR TODAY,
IT WAS CLEAR TODAY—
I WAS HERE TODAY!

AND MAYBE IT'S
THE WHITE MAN'S GAME
DAMMIT!
I CAN PLAY IT, TOO!
I CAN RACE!
I CAN CLIMB!
IT'S THE PLACE!
IT'S THE TIME!
I CAN PLAY!

(*Spoken.*) Rae, they didn't keep me from eating in a restaurant, or make me sit in the back of a bus! They kicked me off a ballfield! That's never happened before! *That's progress!*

ACT ONE

SCENE 9

The Dodger Locker Room at Ebbets Field, Brooklyn.
Upstage left are the lockers, where several DODGERS *are chang-*

ing into THEIR *uniforms. Downstage is a rubbing table, on which is a deck of cards and some money.*

CASEY, HATRACK, SWANEE *and two other* DODGERS *are sitting around the rubbing table on stools — obviously in the middle of a poker game.*

(*MUSIC.*)

IT AIN'T GONNA WORK

CASEY.
RICKEY'S A FLYING FOOL!
　HATRACK.
I THINK HIS BRAIN GOT BENT!
　CASEY.
FRIG THIS EXPERIMENT!
　BOTH.
HELL!
　CASEY.
IT AIN'T GONNA WORK!
THIS AIN'T NO SUNDAY SCHOOL —
　SWANEE.
THIS IS A BASEBALL TEAM —
　CASEY.
RICKEY CAN SHOVE HIS DREAM!
　CASEY, SWANEE and HATRACK.
HELL!
IT AIN'T GONNA WORK!
　HATRACK.
DON'T CARE HOW GOOD WE GET,
　SWANEE.
NO NIGGER'S WORTH THE SWEAT,
　BOTH.
THAT'S SOMETHING RICKEY CAN'T SELL!
　HATRACK.
DON'T CARE HOW LOUD THEY CHEER,
　CASEY.
WE GOT A MINEFIELD HERE —
　ALL THREE.
IT'S GONNA BLOW US TO HELL!
　ALL DODGERS.
RICKEY'S A STUBBORN MULE.
MAYBE HE'S LOST HIS MIND.

CASEY.
MAYBE HE'S COLOR BLIND—!
ALL DODGERS.
HELL! IT AIN'T GONNA WORK!

(*The following dialog is spoken, but underscored.*)

SWANEE. Some spring. Five games cancelled.
HATRACK. Now! We got to do this strike now!
SWANEE. The boys are real ticked off.
HATRACK. Even the ones that didn't sign.
CASEY. We can't call no strike now.
DODGER. Why not?
CASEY. We can't do nothin' till Sambo's made the team. And he ain't made the team.
SWANEE. Yet. It's only a matter of time.
HATRACK. Yeah, it is. He's some ballplayer, ain't he? Did you see that one-handed catch he made . . . ? (HE *sees the* OTHERS *looking at* HIM.) I'm gonna go take my shower.

(*The following is sung:*)

CASEY.
HATRACK!
CAN'T LET THAT NIGGER PLAY!
ROOKIE.
WE GOTTA MOVE
ALL DODGERS.
TODAY!
CASEY.
SEASON'S A WEEK AWAY.
ALL DODGERS.
HELL! IT AIN'T GONNA WORK!
HELL! IT AIN'T GONNA WORK!

(RICKEY *and* LEO *enter the locker room and cross downstage to the rubbing table.* HATRACK *turns and sees them.*)

HATRACK. Mr. Rickey!
CASEY. Mr. Rickey. We're, uh, just havin' a little meetin' on our own makin' sure we've got the signals straight.
SWANEE. Signals. Rights. (SWANEE *demonstrates a compli-*

cated signal. HATRACK *then demonstrates a signal to bunt, which involves a lot of slapping of arms and thighs.*)

LEO. Not bad. I'll remember that the next time I want to get Gene Krupa to bunt.

ROOKIE. (*Wanting to avoid a dangerous situation.*) I'm gonna go hit a few fungoes. Skipper. (HE *leaves hurriedly.*)

RICKEY. Leo what say we use this opportunity to demonstrate some *new* signals. (HE *sees the cards on the rubbing table.*) Cards, gentlemen? With such a strict rule . . . ?

SWANEE. (*Scooping up the money and pocketing it quickly.*) We weren't really gambling, Mr. Rickey. Just penny ante.

RICKEY. Well I suppose gambling is OK if the stakes are right. May we join you?

CASEY. We'd be honored. Wouldn't we boys?

DODGERS. (*Ad lib.*) Sure, Mr. Rickey.

(RICKEY *and* LEO *take stools at opposite ends of the rubbing table.* RICKEY *begins to deftly shuffle the cards.*)

RICKEY. I believe I recall the rules to a few card games.

CASEY. Black Jack? (*The* DODGERS *suppress laughter.*)

LEO. I didn't think you wanted to play that game, Higgins.

RICKEY. You know, Mr. Higgins, the dealer always wins when you play that game. Cut. (SWANEE *cuts.*) How about a hand of five card draw poker? (RICKEY *begins to deal swiftly.*)

CASEY. Whatever. Long as it's accordin' to Hoyle.

SWANEE. What about those new signals you were talking about, Mr. Rickey? The new hit and run?

RICKEY. No. These signals deal with something a bit more universal. A concept known as Historical Inevitability.

CASEY. Beg pardon?

LEO. That means something whose time has come.

RICKEY. Or gone.

(*MUSIC.*)

THE BROOKLYN DODGER STRIKE

RICKEY.
DO YOU REMEMBER D-DAY, LEO?
THE ALLIED ARMIES UNDER IKE.

LEO.
THE WAY HE CAUGHT THEM NAZIS NAPPIN',
AND LET 'EM HAVE IT—
UP THE PIKE!
RICKEY.
THAT WAS A BLOODY DAY, BY GOLLY!
LEO.
BUT IT WAS NEXT TO NOTHING LIKE . . .
BOTH.
THE CASEY HIGGINS,
HATRACK HARRIS,
BROOKLYN DODGER STRIKE.

(*The following section is spoken with underscoring:*)

LEO. When I think of history, I have trouble thinking past last year when one game kept me from cashing a big, fat World Series check.

RICKEY. One game. Cards, gentlemen? Mr. Higgins?

CASEY. I'll stand pat.

LEO. Well, I won't. We've got this guy who can help us win at least ten games.

RICKEY. On his base running alone.

HATRACK. I'll take four.

LEO. I'll take one. Now, I don't care if a guy is pink or purple or striped like a zebra. I'm the manager. I decide who plays.

RICKEY. With my total support. Total support . . . (*Giving* HIMSELF *two cards.*) . . . takes two.

LEO. But some guys think they can keep me from playing this guy. When anybody knows I'd win more games not playing *them.*

RICKEY. It seems they're guilty of incising more than they can masticate.

HATRACK. (*Shocked.*) Mr. Rickey!

LEO. (*Explaining patiently to* HATRACK.) Biting off more than they can chew.

(*The following section is sung:*)

RICKEY.
HISTORY TELLS OF ARMSTRONG CUSTER,
THAT UNION GENERAL FULL OF PRIDE.

Leo.
THOUGHT HE COULD TAME AN INDIAN NATION,
WITH LESS THAN THIRTY ON HIS SIDE.

Rickey.
IT WAS A GROSS MISCALCULATION—
WITH REPERCUSSIONS FAR AND WIDE.

Both.
JUST LIKE THE CASEY HIGGINS,
SWANEE RIVERS,
DOUBLE SUICIDE.

(*The following section is spoken with underscoring:*)

(Each *of the* Dodgers *pass in turn, until the betting comes around to* Rickey.)

Rickey. (*Betting $5.*) Not that this means total disaster.
Casey. (*Seeing the bet.*) No?
Leo. Of course not. Mr. Rickey is a fair-minded man.
Hatrack. I fold. (Leo *sees the bet.*)
Rickey. A wise decision.
Swanee. Out.
Rickey. Now, if any of you gentlemen still believes he has the right to pick and choose his team-mates, I will be only too happy to let him exercise that right.
Dodgers. (*Ad lib.*) Thank you, Mr. Rickey.
Rickey. Just see me privately, and we will examine the rosters of the Philadelphia Athletics and the St. Louis Browns.
Leo. Oh, St. Louis. The Browns are such a thrilling ballclub. And St. Louis is so lovely in the summer. The breeze blowing in off the ocean . . .
Casey. (*Laying down* His *cards.*) There's no ocean in St. Louis. I got a nine high straight.
Leo. There's no breeze either. (*Laying down* His *cards.*) I've got a straight, too. Seven, eight, nine, ten . . .
Rickey. Jack! Gentlemen, I know you are intelligent enough to understand that as the owner of this ballclub, I hold all the cards. (*Laying down* His *cards.*) Flush. All black! (*Picking up the money.*) Mr. Harris, Mr. Rivers, Mr. Higgins. (He *starts to exit, remembers something and returns to the rubbing table.*) Oh, by the way . . .

(*The following section is sung:*)

RICKEY.
THERE ON THE DECK OF THE TITANIC
THE DAUNTLESS CAPTAIN GRABBED THE MIKE.
AND HE APOLOGIZED PROFUSELY—
"WE SIMPLY COULD NOT
PLUG THE DIKE."
AS WE WENT SWIMMING
TOWARD HIS MAKER,
HE SAID . . .
    LEO. (*Snapping* HIS *fingers.*)
YOU KNOW WHAT THIS IS LIKE?
    HATRACK. (*Spoken.*) I know.
    DODGERS. (*Spoken.*) I know.
    SWANEE. (*Spoken.*) I know.
    ALL EXCEPT CASEY.
THE CASEY HIGGINS,
HATRACK HARRIS,
BROOKLYN DODGER
    LEO.
(AIN'T TALKIN' 'BOUT THE PHILLIES)
    ALL EXCEPT CASEY.
BROOKLYN
DODGER
STRIKE!
    LEO. (*Clapping* HIS *hands.*) All right, the fun and games are
over. It's back to baseball!

(*Two* DODGER COACHES *enter and push the rubbing table out of
    the locker area, as* THEY *bring a huge chalk-board in.* ALL
    the DODGERS, *except* CASEY *gather around the chalk-board,
    as* LEO *begins a "chalk-talk" session.* CASEY *stands off to the
    side by* HIMSELF, *obviously deep in thought.* RICKEY *crosses
    to a quiet part of the locker room to have a talk with*
    SUKEFORTH.)

SUKEFORTH. The number assignments are all done. Branca
wanted number thirteen, but Higbe is thirteen, so we gave him
number 20. All the numbers are taken up through forty-one.
    RICKEY. Good, good.
    CASEY. (*Crossing to* RICKEY.) Mr. Rickey, could I talk to you
for a minute?

RICKEY. Certainly. (*To* SUKEFORTH.) Thank you, Sukey.

CASEY. Mr. Rickey, you could sell a sear-sucker suit to a Eskimo, but you ain't sellin' me squat. The sovereign state of Georgia didn't make me go to school with 'em. The US Army didn't make me fight Nazis with 'em. And sure as God made bear shit brown, you can't make me play baseball with 'em.

RICKEY. Mr. Higgins . . .

CASEY. Trade me.

RICKEY. Mr. Higgins, give this a chance. Harris has. And Rivers. Bragan. Dixie Walker.

CASEY. Dixie sent you a letter. You got Dixie's letter.

RICKEY. Yes. And I'm acting on it. However, maneuvering an equitable trade for a player of *his* stature takes time. I'm confident that during that time . . .

CASEY. What about *my* stature? I'm a good pitcher.

RICKEY. Yes, you are. And I want you to continue pitching for the Brooklyn Dodgers.

CASEY. Then don't sign Robinson.

RICKEY. Mr. Higgins, have you considered that negotiating a new contract with a new club at this stage of your career could cost you a great deal of money?

CASEY. My self-respect is more important than money.

RICKEY. (*Truly angered.*) Self-respect! So come October when the season is through, you can walk down Main Street in that pellegra-pit you call home and boast to your chinless kinfolk that instead of winning twenty games with a championship team, you lost twenty games with a group of lily-white losers!?

CASEY. You trade me!

(RICKEY *exits in disgust.* CASEY *walks to the other side of the locker room, where the "chalk-talk" session is in full swing.*)

LEO. Spring training was a piece of cake. You won a lot of ballgames. You're feelin' pretty good, huh? Gettin' a little cocky? (*The* DODGERS *all nod in agreement.*) Well, you got nothin' to get cocky about! The Cards are comin' back with the same team they had last year. And what happened last year?

DODGERS. (*Mumbling.*) They beat us, Skipper.

LEO. They beat us, they beat us. That's right, they beat us. Pittsburgh! We can beat Pittsburgh. Erasmus Hall High School can beat Pittsburgh. The rest of the League is a street fight, and we'd better come out throwin' bricks or I'm gonna kick ass and take names! Rivers. You better watch that hitch in your swing, or you're gonna end up on the bench. And I don't like you well enough to wanna spend 154 games sittin' next to you. (*Moving to the next* DODGER.) Reiser. (HE *holds up one hand.*) This is you. (HE *holds up the other hand.*) This is a wall. (HE *claps* HIS *hands together.*) Reiser, no. Watch yourself. (*Moving to the next* DODGER.) Branca, you're telegraphing your curve. You're . . .

DODGER. Leo. Who's gonna be playing first.

CASEY. Bojangles.

LEO. We got a first-baseman on the team. Now . . .

(SUKEFORTH *enters, holding an official-looking press release.*)

SUKEFORTH. Leo . . .

LEO. Ok, fellows, relax for a minute. (*Crossing to* SUKE-FORTH.) Yeah?

SUKEFORTH. Our Commissioner of Baseball, Happy Chandler, is going to make this public this afternoon.

LEO. (*Reading the paper.*) Good Christ! (LEO *runs from the locker room, with* SUKEFORTH *behind* HIM.)

ACT ONE

SCENE 10

BRANCH RICKEY's *office, a few minutes later.*
RICKEY *is on the phone—angry but trying to be reasonable.*

RICKEY. Mr. Commissioner, this would never stand up in a court of law. What crime has he committed? That is hearsay! That is innuendo! Happy . . . may I call you Happy? It is four days before the season begins. This reeks of vendetta. The other owners are *not* impartial! I am about one inch away from a National League pennant, and of course, they will stop me any way then can. (HE *listens for a moment.*) Very well. (HE *listens for a moment.*) Very well! (HE *hangs up the phone.*) May I call you Happy? Dopey would be more like it!

(LEO *enters in civilian clothes.*)

LEO. Any news?

RICKEY. All bad. I've exhausted every avenue of appeal. Chandler wants to make it stick — trumped charges or no. Never did I expect those closed-minded midgets who run this great game to stoop so low!

LEO. But they have.

RICKEY. Indeed they have. (JACKIE *and* RACHEL *enter.*) Ah, Jack. Rachel. Please sit down. I've asked you here this morning because something absolutely unforeseen has occurred. It affects our plans most directly. (HE *hands* JACKIE *the press release.*) The Commissioner of Baseball will release this today. It will be in tonight's newspapers.

JACKIE. (*Reading.*) "As a result of the accumulation of unpleasant incidents detrimental to baseball, Dodger Manager Leo Durocher . . .

LEO. ". . . is hereby suspended from baseball for the 1947 season."

JACKIE. For what?

LEO. For nothin'!

JACKIE. Can't you do anything?

RICKEY. I've spoken with the Commissioner. But Chandler wants to make it stick.

LEO. Zip. That's what we can do, zip. I'm out of baseball, for a year.

RACHEL. Leo, I'm sorry.

RICKEY. Never in history has the game made so audacious a move. And this affects our plans most directly, Jack. We knew this would be difficult. But without Leo on your side . . .

LEO. . . . and on their backs . . .

RICKEY. . . . it might be impossible. Please take the time to consider what this will mean on the field. Do not answer hastily. Do we wait a year?

JACKIE and RACHEL. (*Quickly.*) No!

JACKIE. No. This is no coincidence. The owners are against us, and look what happens. You're ready to bring me up to the Dodgers, they know that. Leo wants me on the club. They know that. I can't fight back, but he can fight for me. They know that. And now he gets suspended for a year?

LEO. And for what? For nothin'!

RACHEL. Mr. Rickey, we've been waiting for an awfully long time.

RICKEY. Yes, you have.

JACKIE. And if we wait any longer, God only knows what they'll come up with.

RICKEY. You are right. We'll let them have today. Tomorrow, we'll make our own headlines. (RICKEY *takes a contract out of* HIS *desk drawer.* HE *puts the contract on* HIS *desk and hands a pen to* JACKIE. JACKIE *looks at* RACHEL, *who nods that* HE *is doing the right thing. Then,* JACKIE *looks at* RICKEY, *takes the pen and signs the contract. Suddenly,* RICKEY *hugs* JACKIE *impulsively.*)

RICKEY. Jack, welcome to the National League.

(*MUSIC.*)

JACK ROOSEVELT ROBINSON/THE FIRST (Reprise)

RICKEY.
EIGHT MAJOR CITIES—
YOU'LL WIN THE DAY IN EACH ONE!
YOU'LL HAVE THEM CHEERING FOR
JACK ROOSEVELT ROBINSON!

PITTSBURGH TO BOSTON—
THE PRESSURES WILL WEIGH A TON.
BUT WHO'S THE WINNER? IT'S
JACK ROOSEVELT ROBINSON!

LEO. (*Spoken.*) Good luck, Robinson. Give 'em a couple for me!

(JACKIE *shakes* LEO's *hand. Then,* HE *hugs* RACHEL *and leaves the office to go to the stadium.*)

RACHEL.
HIS WHOLE LIFE
HAS BEEN AIMED AT THIS MOMENT.
GOD KNOWS IF IT EVER
COMES AGAIN.
AND THE MOMENT BELONGS
JUST AS MUCH TO HIM
AS IT DOES TO
THE BROTHERHOOD OF MEN.

ACT ONE

SCENE II

A ballfield, seen in silhouette, just before a game. The PLAYERS,
   UMPIRES *and* COACHES *are milling around the field. There is
   an air of nervous anticipation about the moment.*
THEY *form a diagonal line, remove* THEIR *caps and sing:*

ALL.
. . . O'ER THE LAND OF THE FREE
AND THE HOME OF THE BRAVE.

(*As* THEY *run to their respective field positions, we hear over the
   stadium p.a. system:*)

STADIUM ANNOUNCER. . . . would like to welcome you to
this, the opening game of the 1947 National League season.
(*Cheering.*) Ladeez and gentlemen . . . this is the starting line-up
for the Brook-a-lyn Dod-juhs. (*Cheering.*) Batting lead-off,
Numbah twelve, the second baseman, Eddie Stankeeeee. (*Cheering.* EDDIE STANKY *leaves a group of* PLAYERS *and runs to second base.*) Batting in the second po-sition, the short-stop, numbah one, Harold, "Pee Wee," Reeeeese. (*Cheering.* PEE WEE
REESE *leaves the group of* PLAYERS *and runs to short-stop.*) Batting in the third po-sition, the first baseman, numbah forty-two,
Jack Roosevelt Robinson.

(*From the group of* PLAYERS, JACKIE *emerges.* HE *kneels, holding* HIS *bat, in the on-deck circle, and then sprints down to
   first base. Booing is hard from the stands. The booing turns
   to chanting, which grows louder and louder.*)

CROWD.
Jungle bunny! Jigaboo!
Jungle bunny! Jigaboo!
Jungle bunny! Jigaboo!
Jigaboo!
Jigaboo!

(*Suddenly, one voice is heard above the crowd.*)

THE FIRST

ANGRY FAN. Get the nigger off the field!

(*A watermelon is thrown from the stands, which lands at* JACKIE'S *feet, splattering all over the field.* JACKIE *is startled, but holds* HIS *ground.* HE *stands very tall, straighter and prouder and more defiant than* HE *has ever been.*)

AS THE CURTAIN FALLS

END OF ACT ONE

ACT TWO

SCENE 1

The Polo Grounds—home of the New York Giants—in Manhattan. The BROOKLYN DODGERS *are taking batting practice before the game.*

PATSY, HUEY *and* SORRENTINO—*hard-core Dodger Fans—enter the stands and take* THEIR *seats to watch batting practice.* SORRENTINO's *seat is better than* HUEY's *and* PATSY's, *and slightly removed from* THEIR's.

PATSY. Look! That's him! Jackie Robinson!

SORRENTINO. Which one?

HUEY. (*Sarcastically.*) The tall one. (*Consulting* HIS *box scores.*) First month of the season, he's been hittin' like . . .

SORRENTINO. But yesterday, here at the Polo Grounds where it counts? Four times up, four times . . . (HE *gives a "raspberry,"*) Colored guys choke up under pressure. They can't take the competition.

PATSY. (*Nudging* HUEY. BOTH *decide to put on* SORRENTINO.) Oh, yeah. That's a proven fact.

SORRENTINO. Yeah. A proven fact.

PATSY. And you know who proved it? Joe Louis in his second fight with Max Schmeling. (SORRENTINO *nods* HIS *head sagely.*)

HUEY. Oh, my apologies, Sorrentino. I forgot all about that one. Schmeling would have had him, too, if Louis hadn't snuck in four hundred lucky punches.

SORRENTINO. They got their league. That's where they belong.

PATSY. Hey, Sorrentino, look at this. (HUEY *holds up a book for* SORRENTINO *to see.*)

SORRENTINO. "The Official Baseball Book of the Colored Major Leagues."

HUEY. (*Filled with facts, which* HE *knows without reading.*) Othello Renfroe—.404 lifetime batting average. Cool Minnie Edwards—fifty-seven hits in eleven days.

PATSY. And Satchel Paige shut out the Bob Feller All-Stars in 1939, striking out the last three men while sitting in a rocking chair!

(SORRENTINO *is not impressed. The* KANSAS CITY MONARCHS *enter*— JUNKYARD, BUCKY, SOFTBALL, RODNEY, THE EQUIP-MENT MANAGER *and* COOL MINNIE, *with two beauties in tow* — RUBY *and* OPAL. *With much noise and confusion,* THEY *find* THEIR *seats, which happen to surround* SORRENTINO. *After a moment of panic,* SORRENTINO *moves to another part of the stands.* THEY *all watch* JACKIE *field a few grounders.* RUBY *is particularly impressed.*)

RUBY. What a wonderful ballplayer!
COOL MINNIE. 'Course he's wonderful. I taught him everything he knows.
RUBY and OPAL. You what?
RUBY. You talkin' jive again, Minnie?
COOL MINNIE. No, I ain't.
JUNKYARD. Didn't you know that? Top to bottom. A to Z.

(SUKEFORTH *enters the field, calls a halt to batting practice, and calls the* DODGERS *over to* HIM *for instructions.*)

COOL MINNIE. That day in Chicago, I had to take him by the hand down to Union Station and put him on the right train to Brooklyn and glory. I told him, "Jack, there must be fifty boys in the colored league as good as you. But you're the one they picked, and we got to make you look good." So, waitin' for the train, I sat him down and told him all the secrets my grandpappy told me. Secrets *his* grandpappy took here from Africa. (HE *looks* RUBY *right in the eye, and speaks with great solemnity.*) Where baseball was invented. You didn't know that, did you?
RUBY. (*Suspicious.*) What kind of secrets?
COOL MINNIE. How to hit like thunder. And how to run like lightning.
JUNKYARD. When the curve ball is a comin', and when it's a change of pace.
COOL MINNIE. And that boy was so slow and thick-headed, why if the train hadn't been two hours late . . .

(SUKEFORTH *has finished talking with the* DODGERS.)

SUKEFORTH. (*Clapping* HIS *hands.*) All right, fellows, let's go.

(*The Dodgers all begin to trot past the stands to the locker room.* HUEY *and* PATSY *rise to leave the stands.*)

HUEY. C'mon, Patsy. I wanna frankfurter.

(*As* JACKIE *jogs past the stands,* HE *sees the* MONARCHS *waving frantically at* HIM.)

JACKIE. Minnie! Bucky! Softball! What are you guys doing here?
COOL MINNIE. Playing the Newark Eagles tonight.
JUNKYARD. Came to watch you smite the Giants today.
JACKIE. Junkyard!
SORRENTINO. (*Approaching* JACKIE *shyly.*) Could you sign my scorecard, please?
JACKIE. (*To* SORRENTINO.) Sure. (*As* HE *signs the scorecard, to the* MONARCHS.) How are the Monarchs?
BUCKY. Not bad. The owners finally got rid of that rickety old bus.
JACKIE. The one that kept making me car sick? That is good news.
SOFTBALL. We thought so, too. Till we found out we had to walk.

(*All the* MONARCHS *and* JACKIE *laugh.* SORRENTINO *examines* HIS *scorecard.*)

SORRENTINO. (*Handing the scorecard back to* JACKIE.) Uh . . . could you make that, "To my good friend, Sorrentino?" (JACKIE *does so.*)
RUBY. Mr. Robinson, may I ask you a personal question?
JACKIE. Yes.
RUBY. Is it true that Cool Minnie taught you everything you know about playing baseball?

(COOL MINNIE, *standing behind* RUBY, *gestures wildly to* JACKIE *to play along.*)

JACKIE. Everything. How to . . . (COOL MINNIE *pantomimes running.*) . . . run like . . . (COOL MINNIE *pantomimes a thunder storm.*) . . . rain. (COOL MINNIE *shakes* HIS *head, "No."*) . . . thunder. How to hit like . . . (COOL MINNIE *pantomimes lightning.*) . . . lightning.
RUBY. (*To* COOL MINNIE.) I thought you said it was hit like thunder, run like lightning?
COOL MINNIE. I told you he was slow.

JUNKYARD. Jack, you think we could come out on the field?
JACKIE. It's still an hour before the game. Sure.

(*The* MONARCHS *leap from the stands onto the playing field, and then look around in awe.*)

BUCKY. So this is what the major leagues feel like.
SOFTBALL. Jackie Robinson, you got everything. A clean uniform. And a number that you get to keep from game to game to game.
COOL MINNIE. Jack, you are doin' it. Hell, I know it ain't easy, but you're doin' in!
SOFTBALL. Leading the league in stolen bases.
COOL MINNIE. That's a smart man playin'.
JUNKYARD. And in sacrifice hits.
COOL MINNIE. That's a team man playin'.
JACKIE. And in number of times being hit by a pitched ball.
COOL MINNIE. That's a black man playin'.

(*MUSIC.*)

YOU DO, DO, DO IT GOOD!

COOL MINNIE.
YOU ARE THE PRINCE OF FANCY FOOTWORK
YOU ARE THE PUSSYCAT'S MEOW
OTHER MEN KNOW WHO, OR WHAT, OR WHERE
YOU KNOW WHO-WHAT-WHERE-WHEN, PLUS HOW!

YOU'RE AS SHINEY AS A COPPER PENNY
YOU GUSSY UP THE NEIGHBORHOOD
NOT ONLY DO YOU DO IT, JACK
BUT YOU DO-DO-DO IT GOOD!

YOU ARE THE PRIDE OF EV'RY BROTHER,
RIGHT UP THERE WITH BOOKER T.
COOL AS WINTERGREEN,
SLICK AS BRILLIANTINE—
YOU ARE FINE MACHINERY!

LOVE TO SEE YOU ON THOSE BILLBOARDS
THE WAY YOU FLASH THAT TOOTHPASTE SMILE.
NOT ONLY DO YOU GIVE IT HEART

BUT YOU GI-GI-GIVE IT STYLE
RODNEY.
PRETTY LADIES UP IN HARLEM
GONNA LEAVE THEIR SUGAR DADDIES
AN' COME SMOOCH YOU!
MONARCHS.
(SMOOOCH YOU)
BUCKY.
CONGRESSMEN AND GENERALS
JUMP OVER ONE ANOTHER
TO SALUTE YOU!
MONARCHS.
(LOOOCHOOO)
JUNKYARD.
MEN WHO CHEW TOBACCO
GONNA WANNA CHEW
THE SAME TOBACCO YOU CHEW!
MONARCHS.
(YOUCHOOO)
SOFTBALL.
YOU THE ONLY COLORED MAN ALIVE
ALLOWED TO RIDE UPON
THE CHATTANOOGA CHOO-CHOO!
MONARCHS.
(PARDON ME, BOY)

COOL MINNIE	MONARCHS
YOU ARE A GRAND	
ILLUMINATION	YOU'RE GRAND!
IN OTHER WORDS, A SUPER	
STAR—	YOU'RE A STAR!
DESTINED TO BECOME	
A BUBBLE GUM,	
OR BETTER STILL—	
A CHOC'LATE-COVERED	
CANDY BAR!	

MONARCHS.
AND WHEN YOUR PLAYIN' DAYS ARE OVER

COOL MINNIE	MONARCHS
YOU'LL PRO'LLY GO TO	
HOLLYWOOD	HOLLYWOOD!
NOT ONLY DO YOU DO IT,	
JACK	
BUT YOU DO-DO-DO IT GOOD!	

Monarchs.
CHA DO IT GOOD
CHA DO IT GOOD
CHA DO IT GOOD
CHA DO IT . . .

(*DANCE BREAK.*)

Monarchs.
CHA DO-DO-DO IT
  Cool Minnie.
AW, YOU DO-DO-DO IT
  Monarchs.
CHA DO-DO-DO IT
   Cool Minnie.
AW, YOU DO-DO-DO IT
  Monarchs.
CHA DO
CHA DO
CHA DO
CHA DO
CHA DO IT
WHEN YOUR PLAYIN' DAYS ARE OVER

Cool Minnie	Monarchs
YOU'LL PRO'LLY GO TO	
HOLLYWOOD	HOLLYWOOD!
NOT ONLY DO YOU DO IT,	
JACK	

  Monarchs.
BUT CHA DO-DO-DO IT
CHA DO-DO-DO IT
CHA DO-DO-DO (IT)
  Cool Minnie.
ITTTTTTTTTTTTTTTTTTTTTTTTTTTTT.
(He *holds the note for an impossibly long time.*)
  Ruby. (*Spoken.*) Stop that, Minnie. You gonna hurt yourself.
  Cool Minnie.
NOT SO BAD!
  All.
CHA DO-DO-DO IT
GOOD!

ACT TWO

Scene 2

The Dodger Locker room at Shibe Park, Philadelphia, before a game.

Swanee *is on rubbing table, being worked over by a* Trainer. Pee Wee *and a* Rookie *are changing into* Their *"away grays" and* Hatrack *is sitting next to the rubbing table reading — with difficulty — to* Swanee *from the entertainment section of the Philadelphia paper.*

Hatrack. How 'bout "The Best Years of Our Lives?"
Swanee. Nope.
Hatrack. "Destry Rides Again?"
Swanee. No.
Trainer. You guys hear? Sukey got a letter from Durocher? From Paris, France.
Rookie. I always wanted to play for Durocher. He's the best manager the Dodgers ever had.
Trainer. Yeah, he says he's goin' crazy. Nobody to scream at.
Hatrack. (*Still focused on the newspaper.*) How 'bout "Song of Bernadette?"
Swanee. I don't wanna see no musical.

(Trainer *slaps* Swanee *to finish the rub-down, and calls to the* Rookie.)

Trainer. Come on, Bobby, you're next.
Swanee. Philadelphia's just as bad as New York. Ain't nothin' to see tonight.

(Jackie *enters the locker room, crosses to a stool, and begins to put on* His *spikes.* Casey Higgins *enters the locker room, wearing a particularly loud sport jacket.* Swanee *crosses to* Casey *and makes an elaborate show of inspecting the jacket.*)

Swanee. Oh, Casey! Is that what you win when you hit the sign? (*Suddenly,* Swanee *makes a gagging gesture and falls to the floor in disgust over the jacket.* Casey, *unperturbed, then displays the lining of the jacket to the* Dodgers. *The lining is*

even louder than the jacket. The DODGERS *all hoot and groan.*
SUKEFORTH *enters, with* POWERS *in hot pursuit.*)

SUKEFORTH. OK, girls, you're gonna have to break this up.
We've got a little meeting scheduled.

(*The* TRAINER *exits, the* DODGERS *all begin to change into* THEIR
"away grays.")

POWERS. All right, Sukey, what do you know about this
Phillies boycott?
SUKEFORTH. Not very much. Mr. Rickey is on the phone with
the Commissioner's Office right now.
POWERS. And what about this rumored Casey Higgins trade?
SUKEFORTH. You'd better ask Mr. Rickey.
POWERS. I will. (*Crossing to* JACKIE.) Jackie, does Brooklyn
miss Leo Durocher?
JACKIE. Does the army miss General Patton?
SUKEFORTH. (*The good company man.*) But Shotton's doing a
fine job for us.
POWERS. Didn't you want that job?
SUKEFORTH. I had to manage that first game in Boston. I re-
tired, undefeated.
POWERS. (*To* SUKEFORTH.) What happened to you yesterday?
Jackie scores from first on Reiser's single. He comes around
third, and you . . . stand there.
SUKEFORTH. I'll tell you the truth. I couldn't move.
JACKIE. McCormack was playing it deep. He doesn't have
much of an arm. I knew I could beat the throw.
SUKEFORTH. I didn't think so.
JACKIE. I know. I kept looking at you for some kind of a sign.
Stay at third . . . go for it.
SUKEFORTH. I really couldn't move. I've never seen anybody
run like that.

(*A commotion is heard in the hallway — the shouting of* REPORT-
ERS. RICKEY *enters in a sea of* REPORTERS *clamoring for
answers.*)

RICKEY. Gentlemen, gentlemen, please. Six at a time.
POWERS. Mr. Rickey.
RICKEY. Ah, a familiar voice. (*Turning to see* POWERS.) Yes,
Mr. Powers.

POWERS. First . . . are the Dodgers playing today?

RICKEY. Yes, Mr. Powers, we are. Ralph Branca . . . (*Turning to* SUKEFORTH *for confirmation.*) . . . will be our starting pitcher. And Jack Robinson will bat third and play first base.

A REPORTER. But the Phillies actually threatened to walk out?

RICKEY. To be precise, they threatened not to take the field.

ANOTHER REPORTER. Like in St. Louis?

RICKEY. To the best of my knowledge, no. That misguided attempt emanated from the Cardinal players.

POWERS. And the difference?

RICKEY. This morning, the Phillies General Manager, Mr. Herbert Pennock, informed me that his club would not take the field were I to play Jack Robinson. (*Looking at a Philadelphia Reporter's notes.*) There are two N's in Pennock. I responded that I would indeed play Mr. Robinson, and that if the Philadelphias refused to take the field, I would be only too happy to accept a three-game sweep of this series . . . by default.

BLACK REPORTER. Jack. You're playing today?

JACKIE. You bet.

BLACK REPORTER. Does all this pressure affect your playing?

JACKIE. I can't answer that. (*There is a reaction from the* REPORTERS, *indicating that* RICKEY *is keeping a lid on* JACKIE.) The season's only a month old and I've never known anything else.

POWERS. Jackie, what do you do when they throw at you?

JACKIE. The same thing everybody else does. Duck!

(*From the lockers, a quacking sound is heard. It is* CASEY.)

POWERS. Mr. Rickey, Jackie, was there some kind of an incident at the Benjamin Franklin Hotel this morning?

JACKIE. Yes.

RICKEY. No. No incident, Mr. Powers. We were quite matter-of-factly informed that our entire team would not be welcome at the Benjamin Franklin Hotel, and we quite matter-of-factly moved to the twice-as-expensive Warwick. (*Reaction from the* REPORTERS.) Where . . . where *all* the Brooklyn Dodgers will stay on all future trips to the City of Brotherly Love.

POWERS. Mr. Rickey, one final question. There's something that's been bothering me ever since Spring training in Havana.

RICKEY. Yes, Mr. Powers.

POWERS. Mr. Rickey . . .

(*MUSIC.*)

IS THIS YEAR NEXT YEAR?

POWERS. (*Spoken.*)
Is this year next year?
Or is this year last year?
REPORTERS.
AGAIN!
RICKEY. (*Spoken.*)
Well, gentlemen, I . . .
POWERS.
DO YOUR BOYS DELIVA?
REPORTERS.
OR DO WE SIT SHIVA
AGAIN?!
ARE YOU FOREVER BRIDESMAIDS
AND NEVER BRIDES?
IS YOUR FATE DR. JEKYL'S
OR MISTER HYDE'S?
THE BURNING QUESTION
THAT PLAGUES THE FAMILY
OF MEN
IS
IS THIS YEAR NEXT YEAR,
OR IS THIS YEAR LAST YEAR
AGAIN?
RICKEY. (*Spoken.*) Gentlemen, Euell Blackwell can win thirty
games for the Cincinnati Reds. And Stanley Musial can hit .400
for the St. Louis Cardinals. However . . .
(*Sung.*)
WE'LL WIN THE PENNANT QUICKLY
(FORGIVE THE PUN)
AS QUICKLY AS YOU MIGHT SAY
JACK ROBINSON.
DODGERS.
SEPTEMBER COMES UP
AND YOU'LL SEE THE BUMS UP
BY TEN!
RICKEY.
AMEN!
ALL except RICKEY.
HE SAYS THIS YEAR'S NEXT YEAR

(NO IT AIN'T LIKE LAST YEAR)
THE MAN SAYS THIS YEAR'S NEXT YEAR
(NO IT AIN'T LIKE LAST YEAR . . .)

RICKEY. (*Spoken.*) No! The man says, "This year's next year. No, it *isn't* like last year . . .

ALL.
AGAIN!

RICKEY. Thank you, gentlemen, and now we have a game to win today.

> (*The* REPORTERS *exit. A dour little man in a brown suit has stayed behind.* HE *crosses to* RICKEY.)

WATERHOUSE. Mr. Rickey? Brian Waterhouse. (HE *flashes* HIS *FBI badge.*)

RICKEY. Could I see that, again, please. (WATERHOUSE *produces the badge again, and holds it up for* RICKEY'S *inspection.*) Thank you. Jack, could I see you for a moment. Jack, this is Brian Waterhouse of the Philadelphia office of the FBI.

JACKIE. (*Shaking* WATERHOUSE'S *hand.*) Mr. Waterhouse.

> (RICKEY *hands* WATERHOUSE *a letter.* HE *looks it over professionally.*)

WATERHOUSE. This is a hand-written note with no signature and a local post-mark. Any one of two million people could have written it. The odds of finding the guys who . . .

RICKEY. (*Pulling over a stool from the rubbing table.*) Mr. Waterhouse, sit down. (WATERHOUSE *obediently sits.*) I am not asking you to apprehend anyone. I am demanding that you protect the life that the writer of this note so specifically threatens.

JACKIE. Mr. Rickey, I asked you not to do anything about this. I get these all the time.

WATERHOUSE. The boy's right. We see hundreds of these. They don't amount to a hill of beans—most of 'em. Just some lunatic who . . .

RICKEY. Lunatic? Lunatic! May I remind you that sane, well-adjusted people do not go around assassinating first-basemen? And that this particular lunatic does evidence some rather explicit knowledge of this particular baseball stadium. As well as an inordinate expertise in the use of high-powered weaponry.

WATERHOUSE. OK. So, that boils it down to someone who's been in the service and to a ballgame. And someone who doesn't like these . . . changes. Most people would like to see 'em come more gradual.

RICKEY. One was as gradual as I could manage.

JACKIE. Please. Can't we just forget the whole thing?

RICKEY. No we cannot! I have a lot invested in you, Jack.

WATERHOUSE. Then tell him not to play.

RICKEY. That would be tantamount to surrender. Now, let me offer a suggestion. Men at each entrance. A man in the press-box. Two men atop the scoreboard . . . (WATERHOUSE, *fed up with being told what to do, gets up to leave*.) I have not finished yet! (WATERHOUSE, *startled, sits down*.) . . . two men atop the scoreboard, with instructions to be on the lookout—that is the phrase, isn't it?—for someone who might be smuggling in a high-powered weapon. That shouldn't be too difficult. Most of the fans will be in shirt sleeves.

WATERHOUSE. But . . .

RICKEY. The game begins at 2:30. I'll expect you and your men here at 1:00. (WATERHOUSE *wears* HIS *reluctance rather plainly*.) If you need authorization, I can call my friend, John.

WATERHOUSE. John?

RICKEY. Hoover. (WATERHOUSE *exits, disgruntled*. RICKEY *turns to* JACKIE.) Jack, I don't think you should play today.

JACKIE. Mr. Rickey, that would be tantamound to surrender.

SUKEFORTH. (*Rousting the* DODGERS.) OK, fellows, it's that time. Let's get moving.

(*The* DODGERS *collect* THEIR *gloves and equipment, and prepare to leave the locker room.*)

RICKEY. I'm serious.

JACKIE. So am I. That's why I think it's crazy for us to try to stop it. If anybody really wanted to do it, it would be the easiest thing in the world.

RICKEY. This has to frighten you.

JACKIE. A little.

RICKEY. Then how do you play?

JACKIE. (*Grinning*.) Pretty darn good. (JACKIE *starts to exit, but is stopped by* PEE WEE.)

PEE WEE. You missed a couple yesterday. I think it's because you're playing first base like you were still playing short-stop.

JACKIE. No offense.

PEE WEE. You're grabbing the ball with both hands. Why

don't you try stretching for it with one hand? Well . . . try it.

JACKIE. Thanks, Pee Wee.

(SUKEFORTH *enters the locker room with a telegram, which* HE *hands to* RICKEY. *The* DODGERS *are all walking from the locker room.* RICKEY *calls to* CASEY.)

RICKEY. Mr. Higgins, might I trouble you for a moment?

CASEY. (*Jogging back to* RICKEY.) Sure, Mr. Rickey.

RICKEY. Mr. Higgins, I would like to express my gratitude to you—in advance—for affording me one of the few moments of absolutely unadulterated joy I shall experience in my lifetime.

CASEY. Which is?

RICKEY. Mr. Higgins, you are joining the ranks of such baseball immortals as Wilbert Robinson, Zachariah Wheat and Adolph Bisonette. You are about to become a *former* member of the Brooklyn Dodgers. You're gone! Traded! Fired! Pick one! I want you out of my uniform, out of my life, and out of my sight!

CASEY. Where'm I goin'?

RICKEY. I would love to send you to the very edge of this continent. To a city out of Dante's Hell, where summer is an inferno and the air itself is unfit to breathe. However, we do not play major league baseball in Los Angeles.

CASEY. Where'm I goin'!?

RICKEY. Pittsburgh!

(RICKEY *hands* CASEY *the telegram and exits.*)

ACT TWO

SCENE 3

Immediately following the previous scene, in a mesh corridor leading from the locker room to the playing field.

The DODGERS *are crossing through the corridor on* THEIR *way to the field.* JACKIE *trails the group.* CASEY *enters the corridor and calls to* JACKIE.

CASEY. Well, you got your wish. (JACKIE *looks around to see to whom* CASEY *is speaking.*) I'm talking to you, boy!

JACKIE. I don't know what you're talking about.

CASEY. Hell you don't. Rickey traded me today.

JACKIE. I didn't know that.

CASEY. Shit, you didn't. You know how many years I've been on this team? It's my life, boy. Gone to make room for some nigger! (CASEY *spits on* JACKIE, *and throws down* HIS *glove—fists clenched.*) Come on, you black bastard! Rickey ain't here to protect you! (CASEY *circles* JACKIE. HE *lunges, but* JACKIE *easily steps out of* HIS *way.* CASEY *swings at* HIM. *Again,* JACKIE *steps out of the way, but this time* HE *drops* HIS *glove, preparing to fight back.* CASEY *rushes at* JACKIE. JACKIE *grabs* CASEY's *arms, overpowers* HIM, *and pushes* CASEY *against the mesh.*)

JACKIE. You don't want to talk to me, don't talk to me! You don't want to look at me, don't look at me! But, Higgins, there isn't anything you can do to keep me from playing baseball. (HE *releases a defeated and humiliated* CASEY. JACKIE *picks up* HIS *glove, and walks slowly to the playing field, leaving* CASEY *alone.*)

ACT TWO

SCENE 4

A section of the stands at Ebbets Field, just before a game. RACHEL *is sitting alone. Several rows behind* HER *sits* MRS. FURILLO.
RICKEY *enters and walks over to the women.*

RICKEY. Mrs. Furillo . . . Mrs. Robinson. Ah, it's days like this —a clear August afternoon, the team fighting for first place, the Giants here to play—that I truly wish that Ebbets Field had 200,000 seats. (*To* RACHEL.) Rachel, Mrs. Rickey tells me you've found an apartment.

RACHEL. Finally. It's just a one bedroom. But it's in a nice neighborhood—on Tilden Avenue. But, Mr. Rickey, we looked for three months. It's impossible to find an apartment in New York city, even at $60.00 a month.

MRS. STANKY. (*Entering and sitting beside* MRS. FURILLO.) Hello, Mr. Rickey.

RICKEY. Mrs. Stanky. (*To* RACHEL.) How is Jack doing?

RACHEL. He's hitting .319. He's . . . Some days, he's just

perfect. And some . . . I know it's because he can't fight back on the field, but he's like a powder keg. The pressure builds and builds . . .

RICKEY. Rachel, remind him it isn't forever. I'm very proud of him, Rachel. Very proud.

UMPIRE. (*Crossing the field.*) Play Ball!

RACHEL. So am I.

RICKEY. (*Begins to leave, then turns back to the* WOMEN.) The sportswriters have announced a new award which will be given at the season's end — Rookie of the Year. My spies have assured me that if he maintains his present pace, Jack is a shoe-in. (*More to* MRS. FURILLO *and* MRS. STANKY *than to* RACHEL.) Who knows? Maybe even Most Valuable Player. Ladies. (RICKEY *leaves. The* WOMEN *all look out onto the field. From* MRS. STANKY's *reaction, it is apparent that* HER *husband is at bat. The crack of a bat is heard.*)

RED BARBER. (*Heard over the stadium public address system.*) . . . and Stanky is thrown out at first. Not a close play at all. The Brat hasn't really gotten any good wood on anything thrown at him today.

(MRS. STANKY *shifts in* HER *seat, not wanting to look at the other* WIVES. MRS. FURILLO *indicates that* HER *husband is at bat. The crack of a bat is heard.*)

RED BARBER. . . . and Furillo hits a high pop over to 3rd base. Rigney settles under it . . . and makes the catch.

(MRS. FURILLO *angrily grabs a bag of peanuts, and begins to crunch them loudly.* SHE *looks at Mrs. Stanky, but not at* RACHEL. RACHEL *looks lovingly in the direction of home plate. It is obvious that* JACKIE *is at bat. The crack of a bat is heard.*)

RED BARBER. . . . Robinson bunts! Oh, Doctor, it's a good one . . . And Rigney can't get him. The throw to Mize is too late. Robbie beats it out for a base hit!

(MRS. STANKY *and* MRS. FURILLO *stare daggers at* RACHEL. SHE *turns to* THEM, *nods, and turns back to write, "Bunt single" on* HER *scorecard.* SHE *smiles to* HERSELF.)

(*MUSIC.*)

THERE ARE DAYS

RACHEL.
SOMETIMES
THE SUNSHINE'S SHINING,
SOMETIMES
IT'S HURRICANES.
SOMETIMES
A SILVER LINING,
SOMETIMES
JUST ACHES AND PAINS.
MOST TIMES
YOU PAY THE PIPER,
BUT SOMETIMES—
THE PIPER PAYS.
THERE ARE DAYS,
AND THERE ARE DAYS,
AND THERE ARE DAYS.

SOMETIMES
YOUR MAN'S ON TARGET,
SOMETIMES
HE'S OUT OF LINE.
SOMETIMES
HE'S MIGHTY FROSTY,
SOMETIMES
HE'S MIGHTY FINE.
MOST TIMES
HE'S GARY COOPER,
BUT SOMETIMES—
HE'S GABBY HAYES.
THERE ARE DAYS,
AND THERE ARE DAYS,
AND THERE ARE DAYS.
YOU'VE GOT TO LOOK FOR THE LIGHT
OR THE BLUES IN THE NIGHT
WILL UNSETTLE YOUR SOUL.
YOU'VE GOT TO HOPE FOR THE BEST
OR THE WITCH OF THE WEST
WILL COME DIG YOU A HOLE.

'CAUSE
SOMETIMES
THE WORLD'S YOUR OYSTER,
SOMETIMES
IT'S JUST A CLAM.
SOMETIMES
YOU GIVE UP EASY,
SOMETIMES
YOU GIVE A DAMN.
ONE DAY
YOU'RE BUTTERFINGERS,
MONDAY
YOU'RE TRIPLE PLAYS,
THERE ARE DAYS
AND THERE ARE DAYS . . .

(*The crack of a bat is heard.*)

RED BARBER. Robinson rips a line drive past Buddy Kerr. My goodness! That's two singles, a double and a stolen base for Jackie today!
RACHEL.
AND THERE ARE DAYS

(SHE *looks back at the two* WIVES, *writes in* HER *scorecard and smiles as THE LIGHTS FADE OUT.*)

ACT TWO

SCENE 5

The long, wooden front porch of an old, Victorian farmhouse outside St. Louis, Missouri, late in August.
It is night. The moon casts shadows onto the porch from a huge oak tree which seems to envelop the porch.
JACKIE *is talking on the telephone.*

JACKIE. . . . It *was* in the papers. That's why I called, Momma. I thought you might be worried . . . No, I can afford it. I'm calling from St. Louis, not Brooklyn. It's a lot closer . . . No, I'm fine. You know how the papers exaggerate. It was just a little cut. (HE *is lying to* HIS *mother, and uncomfortable about it.*) No, they're a good team. They play hard . . . He came at me because I'm on the other team, not because . . . I *know* that's what the papers are saying, that's why I called. (*Pronouncing the name slowly.*) Ga-ra-gi-o-la. He's a catcher. No, I think he's Italian. (*Trying desperately to change the subject.*) How's Mack? . . . He is? (RACHEL *enters, in quite a different mood from* JACKIE's.) Yes, they're treating me fine. The other day they asked me to play cards . . . No, I didn't gamble. . . (HE *looks imploringly at* RACHEL, *and hands* HER *the telephone.* RACHEL *sits in a rocking chair and talks calmly to Momma.* JACKIE *paces the porch nervously.*)

RACHEL. Yes, Momma. It's lovely here . . . No, Momma, he didn't. Yes, we're fine . . . Yes, we love you, too . . . What, Momma? Yes, we will. Good-bye, Momma. (SHE *hangs up the phone and turns to* JACKIE.) Before we leave St. Louis, we really should buy the Carters a little gift. They've made up feel so at home. I haven't had homemade peach ice cream since I was a little girl.

JACKIE. I'd trade my dignity any day for a dish of ice cream.

RACHEL. What?

JACKIE. (*Giving full vent to* HIS *anger.*) I am an alleged member of the Brooklyn Dodgers! They are at the Chase Hotel in uptown St. Louis, and we are at some minister's home in the middle of the Missouri jungle, and you're going on like it's some kind of Sunday school picnic. Peach ice cream! (HE *swats at a mosquito.*)

RACHEL. Jack! Who are you getting angry with?

JACKIE. You're right, Rae. I'm sorry.

RACHEL. *I* like colored people.

JACKIE. Oh?

RACHEL. Some of my best friends are colored.

JACKIE. Excuse me?

RACHEL. (*Rising and crossing to* JACKIE.) Not only that, when I was a little girl, we had this colored lady who practically raised me. She did the cooking, she did the cleaning, she did the laundry and made sure we did our homework and got to school on time.

JACKIE. Really, what did you call her?

RACHEL. Momma.

JACKIE. OK. OK.

RACHEL. (*Crossing behind* JACKIE *and putting* HER *arms*

around HIM.) I didn't know they asked you to play cards. Who?

JACKIE. Nobody. It was a lie. It was all a lie. (*A pause.*) Rae, be honest. What if I just up and quit.

RACHEL. Are you crazy? Why now? When you're doing so well.

JACKIE. That's why! A month ago I was too proud to quit. To even think about quitting. But, Rae, I've done it. (*A horn honks.*)

RACHEL. Mr. Rickey is here.

JACKIE. (*Yelling after* HER *as* SHE *walks into the yard to greet* RICKEY.) I've hit in twenty-one straight games. I've brought the team up from fifth place. I've proved I can play in anybody's league, and they've proved they don't want me. They don't want me to play their God-damned game, so let 'em have it! (JACKIE *sits angrily in the rocker.* RICKEY *enters, kisses* RACHEL *and rushes eagerly to the porch.*)

RICKEY. Robinson, Robinson! Ah, Robinsons. Rachel, Jack . . . (*Seeing the look on* JACKIE's *face.*) Have I come at a bad time?

JACKIE. No, this is a fine time.

RICKEY. Is something wrong?

JACKIE. Wrong? The food is good, the sheets are clean. And such a lovely location! (HE *swats a mosquito.*)

RICKEY. I see.

JACKIE. (*Crossing down off the porch.*) You don't!

RACHEL. Mr. Rickey, Jack is . . . thinking about . . .

JACKIE. Go ahead, say it!

RACHEL. Jack is thinking about quitting.

RICKEY. When you're doing so well.

JACKIE. And it doesn't mean diddly. You know what they want? They want me to stand on first-base, take a lead-off, roll my eyes and shout, "Feets, don't fail me now!" They want me to wish I was white. Well, I'll tell you something. I never wished I was white.

RICKEY. Well, I'll tell you something. If I'd been in your shoes, I never would have made it out of Florida.

JACKIE. Then why did you think *I* could do it?

RICKEY. Because you have more guts than I have.

JACKIE. (*Crossing to* RACHEL.) And Rae gets her share, too. Yesterday there was some guy in the stands, screaming, "nigger," at the top of his lungs. And Rae was sitting right behind him.

RACHEL. But you got two hits, and we won!

JACKIE. I used to think that would be enough. All it'd take would be a few base hits. Now, I don't know.

RICKEY. Is it something specific?

JACKIE. Specific? You mean like when I'm on base and my team-mate Dixie Walker hits a home-run, and I jog into the dug-out to save him the embarrassment of having to shake my hand? Or Hugh Casey, your ace reliever, stopping a locker room poker game cold to come over and rub my head for luck? No, it's nothing specific.

RACHEL. What do you want, Jack?

JACKIE. For the screams to goddamn stop. That once I proved I could play ball, they'd just let me play ball. I don't expect the guys on the other teams to quit hollering nigger. But I do expect the guys on my team — my team — to say, "Hey, Jack, let's go get a beer." Or, "Hey, I'm sorry they're not letting you stay at the hotel." Instead, I'm some kind of sideshow freak. I just want to be another ballplayer. (JACKIE *crosses down off the porch and sits on' the steps.*)

RICKEY. But Jack, you can never be just another ballplayer. If you leave baseball tomorrow, or retire in ten years with a ticket to the Hall of Fame, you can never undo what you've done. You will *always* be the first.

RACHEL. (*Sensing that* RICKEY *needs to speak to* JACKIE *alone.*) Mr. Rickey, I'll go put up some coffee. (SHE *exits into the house.*)

RICKEY. (*Sitting beside* JACKIE *on the steps.*) Do you remember Larry Doby?

JACKIE. Sure. Big kid. Couldn't hit lefties. I played against him in the colored league. He's with the Newark Eagles.

RICKEY. No longer. Bill Veeck has signed him. Doby joins the Cleveland Indians this weekend. He tried to reach you by phone this afternoon, but you were playing. I promised I would relay a message. He said, and I quote, "I'm scared to death, but thank you."

(JACKIE *and* RICKEY *look at each other for a moment.* JACKIE'*s emotions are strong, but confused. Although this is, in fact, the moment* HE *has waited for,* HE *must now give up* HIS *singularity in the major leagues.*)

(*MUSIC.*)

IT'S A BEGINNING

RICKEY.
IT'S A BEGINNING.
IT DOES COME LATE, I GRANT YOU.
STILL, A BEGINNING.
AND YOU CAN FEEL IT, CAN'T YOU?
FEEL THE RESULT
OF OUR LITTLE HANDSHAKE
FEEL HOW, BY GOD!
YOU HAVE MADE
THE LAND SHAKE.

IT'S A BEGINNING
A DOOR'S BEGUN TO OPEN
BUT WE'LL KEEP WORKING
TIL THERE ARE NONE TO OPEN.
JUST LIKE PLAYING AND WINNING,
IT'S SO GOOD FOR THE HEART.
IT'S A BEGINNING . . .
IT'S A START.

(RACHEL *enters from the house.*)

RACHEL. What did I miss?
JACKIE. The Cleveland Indians signed Larry Doby.
RACHEL. Oh, my God! Oh, Jack . . . Mr. Rickey . . . this is
what it's all been about.
RACHEL.
IT'S A BEGINNING.
A DREAM THAT NEEDS DEFENDING.
BLESSED BEGINNING,
IT MUST NOT KNOW AN ENDING
SLOWLY WE'LL GROW
SLOWLY WE'LL FLOWER
PROUDLY WE'LL GO
FROM THIS UNCERTAIN HOUR.
RACHEL and RICKEY.
IT'S A BEGINNING
A DOOR'S BEGUN TO OPEN
AND WE'LL KEEP WORKING

TIL THERE ARE NONE TO OPEN
  RICKEY.
JUST LIKE PLAYING AND WINNING
  RACHEL.
IT'S SO GOOD FOR THE HEART
IT'S A BEGINNING
  RICKEY.
IT'S A START.

RICKEY. (*Spoken.*) Goodnight, Robinsons. Jack, I'll see you tomorrow at—ah, the irony—Sportsman's Park. Goodnight, son. (RICKEY *exits.* RACHEL *goes to* JACKIE *and pulls* HIM *down beside* HER *on the porch steps.*)

RACHEL. OK, Jack Roosevelt Robinson. You want to do something? I'll tell you what to do. You want to fight back? I'll tell you how to fight back. The next time you grab that bat of yours, you swing it as hard as you can—at the ball! You want to explode? Go ahead! Explode on the basepaths, turning singles into doubles and doubles into triples! You don't like the way they holler, "Nigger?" Well, you be the best ballplayer they've ever seen, and you won't be able to hear the "Nigger" for the cheers.

JACKIE. You sound like Mr. Rickey.

RACHEL. You need to scream at somebody, scream at me. You need to hit somebody, hit me. Not too hard! But when you're out there on the field, there's only one thing you can do—play ball. And there's only one way you can play—the way black people have always had to do everything. Better!

JACKIE. (*Taking* HER *in* HIS *arms.*) I love you, Rachel.

RACHEL. I'm going in. Come.

JACKIE. In a minute. In a minute.

(THEY *kiss.* RACHEL *exits into the house, looking back once to be sure that* JACKIE *is all right.*)

JACKIE. (*Sings.*)
IT'S A BEGINNING
AS CLEAR AS SUMMER LIGHTNING
LIKE ALL BEGINNINGS
SO HOPEFUL, YET SO FRIGHTNING.
ONE DAY YOU FEEL
ALL ALONE AND LONELY
NEXT DAY YOU FIND
THE FIRST IS NOT THE ONLY.

IT'S A BEGINNING
GOD BLESS YOU, LARRY DOBY
(*Looking to Heaven.*)
HELP HIM HIT LEFTIES
OR THEY'LL TRADE HIM TO NAIROBI.
THESE ARE UNCHARTED WATERS
LORD, WILL YOU BE MY CHART?
IN THIS BEGINNING,
A FINE BEGINNING,
IT'S A BEGINNING
LET IT START.

(JACKIE *exits into the house.*)

ACT TWO

SCENE 6

Outside Ebbets Field in Brooklyn. It is late afternoon, just before the pennant winning game with the Pittsburgh Pirates.
In the background, seen through the "Players' Entrance" fence, is Ebbets Field. Several concessionaires are vending buttons and pennants.
Four FANS — HUEY, PATSY, SORRENTINO *and* HILDA CHESTER *(the most loyal and vocal of all Brooklyn fans) — enter.* HUEY *is looking with horror at a newspaper.*

HUEY. Oh, my God!
PATSY, SORRENTINO and HILDA. (*Rushing over to* HUEY.) What? Whatsa matta? What happened?
HUEY. Reiser ran into another wall in St. Louis. He's finished!
PATSY. He's finished? We're finished! We got no bench.
HILDA. It's OK. Pistol Pete'll get better!
PATSY. Yeah. That was the Brooklyn Eagle's report, anyway. A scandal sheet! What's in the Daily News?
HUEY. What's in the Daily News? I'll tell you what's in the Daily News! (*Reading.*) We're in second place. The Cardinals are leading the league. And look who Rickey's gonna play! LOOK!

(*MUSIC.*)

THE OPERA AIN'T OVER

ALL.
IT'S BEEN A NUTTY SEASON!
IT AIN'T BEEN KOSHER!
A COLORED GUY ON FIRST—
AND NO DUROCHER!
    HILDA.
WE GOT A BENCH
AS STRONG AS
A WET WALNETTO.
    ALL.
SO WHO DOES RICKEY PLAY?
WHO DOES RICKEY PLAY?
COOKIE LAVAGETTO!
    SORRENTINO. (*Striding operatically forward and singing ala "Pagliacci."*)
COOKIE LAVAGETTO
HE PLAYS COOKIE LAVAGETTO!
WHO THE HELL IS . . .
LAVAGETTO!
OH, OH, OH, OH, OH!

(SORRENTINO *falls into an operatic collapse.* HUEY, PATSY *and* HILDA *rush to* HIM *and sing the following to revive* HIM. THEY *are joined by other, curious,* FANS, *until by the end of the song, the stage is filled with* FANS.)

    ALL.
WE'RE CHASIN' THE CARDINALS—
THEY'RE FOUR GAMES AHEAD
BUT SOON WE'LL BE CLIPPIN'
THEIR WINGS!

WE'RE FOUR GAMES BEHIND.
BUT THAT DON'T MEAN WE'RE DEAD—
'CAUSE THE OPERA AIN'T OVER
TILL THE FAT LADY SINGS!
    SORRENTINO. (*Spoken.*) More. More.
    ALL.
THE PIRATES AND PHILLIES
THEY AIN'T IN THE RACE

THE GIANTS, THEIR STREAK'S
GONNA SNAP!
    SORRENTINO. (*Pointing to three* BLACK FANS.) I wanna hear
them.
    BLACK FANS.
IT'S GREAT EXPECTATIONS
ALL OVER THE PLACE.
    ALL.
'CAUSE THE CURTAIN STAYS UP
TILL SHE CLOSES HER TRAP.
MIRACLES HAPPEN IN FLATBUSH
    HUEY.
MY AUNT SOPHIE'S KID
GREW KITTENS ON A CAT BUSH.
    ALL.
THE FANS IN CHICAGO
ARE SLITTIN' THEIR THROAT,
BUT HERE HOPE ETERNALLY SPRINGS.
YOU GOTTA REMEMBER
WHAT EURIPEDES WROTE—
THE OPERA AIN'T OVER
    HUEY.
(IT MIGHTA BEEN SHAKESPEARE)
    SOME FANS.
I THINK IT WAS KIPLING
    OTHER FANS.
YOU'RE RIGHT, IT WAS KIPLING.
    PATSY.
I THOUGHT IT WAS SHELLEY!
    SORRENTINO. (*Reviving miraculously and speaking.*) Hey!
Shelley moved to Rego Park!
    ALL.
TIL THE BIG, FAT LADY SINGS!

(JACKIE *and* RACHEL *enter with the Brooklyn Dodgers. The*
    FANS *spot the team and rush to* THEM. *From the opposite di-*
    rection, COOL MINNIE *enters with* RUBY *and* OPAL. JACKIE
    spots COOL MINNIE *and goes over to* HIM.)

    JACKIE. Minnie, you son-of-a-gun! Why didn't you tell me
you were coming to New York?
    COOL MINNIE. Come to see you win a pennant.

(CASEY HIGGINS, *now pitching for Pittsburgh, enters and saunters over to* JACKIE *and* RACHEL.)

CASEY. Well, Jack-boy. I'd be a downright liar if I didn't tell you how much I been lookin' forward to this very moment ever since Rickey sent me to Pittsburgh. I'll be seein' you inside, Jackboy. I'm the one who'll be throwin' against you, tonight. Or near you, if you know what I mean? (*Tipping* HIS *cap to* RACHEL.) Miz Robinson. (CASEY *goes into the stadium.* HILDA CHESTER *begins to clang* HER *cowbell for attention.*)

HILDA. (*Sings.*)
IT'S DOWN TO THE WIRE,
AND UP TO THE BOYS,
TO PUT BROOKLYN BACK ON THE MAP.
TRUE?
　　DODGERS.
TRUE!
　　HILDA.
THE PIRATES ARE HAS-BEENS
THEY AIN'T NOTHIN' BUT NOISE
OH, YOU'LL GIVE IT TO THEM
WITH A ZETZ
　　DODGERS.
AND A ZAP!
　　HILDA. (*Seeing* RICKEY *enter.*) Mr. Rickey!
　　ALL.
WE'RE ROOTIN' FOR RICKEY
TO GO ALL THE WAY
WE GOT THE CHAMPAGNE
IN THE FRIDGE.
　　RICKEY.
I PROMISE A PENNANT
BY THE END OF THE DAY
　　ALL.
YOU BETTER BE RIGHT
OR IT'S RIGHT OFF THE BRIDGE!
SHOUT IT FROM HERE
TO GOWANUS—
THAT THE YEAR
THAT'S KNOWN AS NEXT YEAR
IS UPON US!

(RICKEY *signals for the* DODGERS *to get ready for the game.* THEY *jog into Ebbets Field. In voice-over we hear:*)

RED BARBER. Ralph Branca will be pitching for Brooklyn today. For Pittsburgh, high-powered Casey Higgins. A hometown victory over the Pirates—who are fighting to stay out of the cellar—clinches the cat-bird seat for the Brooklyn Dodgers. But remember, friends, the opera ain't over til the fat lady sings!

ALL.
TODAY WE COULD CLINCH IT!
WE WIN AND—
SHAZZAM!

HILDA.
A FLAG . . .
(SHE *crosses downstage, stepping over several* FANS. *Spoken.*)
Excuse me. (*Sings.*)
. . . FOR THE BOROUGH OF KINGS.

ALL.
YEAH!
BUT WE CAN'T GET TOO COCKY,
'CAUSE IN BASEBALL, MADAM,
THE OPERA AIN'T OVER
THE OPERA AIN'T OVER
THE OPERA AIN'T OVER
THE OPERA AIN'T OVER
THE OPERA AIN'T OVER
TILL THE BIG
FAT
LADY
SINGS
OPERA AIN'T OVER
TILL THE BIG, FAT LADY SINGS!

(*The* FANS *follow* RICKEY *inside Ebbets Field, chanting as* THEY *go:*)

ALL.
GO BUMS!
GO BUMS!
GO BUMS!
GO BUMS!

ACT TWO

SCENE 7

Inside Ebbets Field, the bottom of the seventh inning. CASEY
HIGGINS *is pitching to* JACKIE ROBINSON.
RED BARBER *describes the action over the stadium p.a. system,*
which we see unfolding before us.
The audience in the theatre has become the fans at Ebbetts Field.
Brooklyn Dodger banners and bunting surround the audi-
ence.

RED BARBER. Higgins shakes off a sign from his catcher, Dixie
Howell. He's been throwing fire all afternoon. He delivers . . .
Strike two! He just nicked the inside corner, letter-high. Jack
Robinson didn't even bat an eye-lash. Here's the next pitch . . .
Robinson goes down! I don't believe he's hit. No . . . he doesn't
appear to be hurt. Jackie dusts himself off, steps back into the
box, holding his bat high over his right shoulder. He's ice up
there. And he bunts! The Pirates are caught flat-footed. Higgins
is furious! He can't do anything but hope it rolls foul . . . and it
doesn't. Jackie Robinson is safe at first. Oh, oh. Jackie may
have twisted his ankle coming into the bag. The fans here are
stone quiet as Jackie limps back to first base. He's called for
time. Coach Sukeforth comes across the field. Jackie's trying to
shake it off. He's still limping, but he says he'll play. Swanee
Rivers—0 for 2 so far today—comes up to bat. Jackie takes his
lead off first—visibly favoring his left foot. Hank Greenberg
holds the bag against him.
GREENBERG. You all right? You think you should run on that?
JACKIE. Not only should I run on it, but I should get the 1947
Academy Award for the best faking of an injury against a Pittsburgh pitcher!
RED BARBER. Jackie takes off like a bullet! Oh, doctor! Higgins fires it to second, but Basinski and Cox are nowhere near
second-base. The ball goes out into center field, and Jackie just
strolls into third. It's cat and mouse time as Jackie dances down
off third. Higgins checks him. Jackie's stolen home three times
so far this year, and Casey Higgins knows it. And so do the
32,000 fans here at Ebbets Field who are on their feet and going
numb. And here's the pitch . . . and it's a wild one! Higgins covers home, he gets the toss from Howell, and here comes Jackie
Robinson. Higgins can't make the tag. He's head over heels. The

ball pops out of his glove, and the Brooklyn Dodgers take the lead one to nothing!

(CASEY *picks up the dropped ball, and walks back to the pitchers' mound in disgust. A huge scoreboard covers the playing field. We see* JACKIE'S *one run in the bottom of the seventh appear on the un-automatic scoreboard. Then, we see a zero in the top of the eighth inning, and then, a zero in the bottom of the eighth inning.*)

ACT TWO

SCENE 8

Inside Ebbets field, the top of the ninth inning. The Pittsburgh Pirates are at bat.

JACKIE *is at first-base,* PEE WEE *is at short-stop, and* SWANEE RIVERS *is in the outfield.*

The scene is in silhouette, and in silence. The only sound is the crack of a bat.

A ball is hit. It is a line-drive. SWANEE *picks it off easily.* PEE WEE *signals, "One away."*

A ball is hit. The PLAYERS *follow the ball into deep center field, where it is caught.* PEE WEE *signals, "Two away."*

A ball is hit. PEE WEE *waves off* SWANEE, *settles under the ball and catches it.* HE *holds up the ball in triumph! The game is over. The Brooklyn Dodgers have won the pennant!*

SUKEFORTH *rushes onto the field and hugs* PEE WEE. *Other* DODGERS *begin to run onto the field, hugging, kissing and throwing their gloves in the air in triumph.*

JACKIE *takes a tentative step toward the jubilant ball players, then stops, unsure.* HATRACK HARRIS *rushes from home plate, and throws* HIS *arms around* JACKIE. HATRACK *sees whom* HE *is hugging and steps back.*

Then, HE *looks at* JACKIE *and hugs* HIM *again and lifts* HIM *into the air. The other* PLAYERS *surround* JACKIE, *pulling* HIM *into* THEIR *midst.*

The FANS *rush onto the field.* BALL PLAYERS, FANS, COACHES— *black and white—all become one huge mass of hugging, cheering, jumping Brooklyn winners. As . . .*

THE CURTAIN FALLS

THE END

PROPERTIES AND FURNITURE

ACT ONE

PROLOGUE:
THE PLAYING FIELD   No props or furniture

SCENE 1:
GALLAGHER'S
RESTAURANT
     Bar unit with appropriate bar
         dressing
     Table with three chairs and three
         place settings
     Three glasses with liquid
     Dressing: coffee pot/cups/menus
     Behind Photo Wall: Bread bas-
         ket with bread
     Reporter's pad and pencil
         (Stage Left)
     1947 Flash camera and bulbs
         (Stage Left)

SCENE 2:
THIRD BASE LINE
COMISKY PARK,
  CHICAGO   Bats/Balls/Gloves

SCENE 3:
MONARCH LOCKER
  ROOM
     Towels in all lockers
     One long bench
     Two short stools
     One pair of shoes with shoe
         shine kit
     Dressing: equipment bags/
         mirrors/combs
     Clothes hamper with mop
         (Stage Left)

SCENE 4:
UNION STATION,
  CHICAGO
     Assorted luggage for passengers
         (Stage Left)
     One soldier's duffle bag
         (Stage Left)

Luggage cart with luggage
(Stage Right)
Lady's overnight bag
(Stage Right)
Lady's round hat-box
(Stage Right)

SCENE 5:
RICKEY'S OFFICE

Desk with intercom/phone/
pens/ink blotter
Baseball on desk
Cigar humidifier
Ashtray/matches
Large ledger book
Swivel chair

SCENE 6:
HAVANA TRAINING
CAMP

Petition (Stage Left)
Reporters' pads and pens
(Stage Left)
Ball cart with 13 bats/balls/
gloves

SCENE 7:
OUTSIDE A BALLPARK
JACKSONVILLE,
FLORIDA

Equipment cart with rakes &
shovels (Stage Right)
Paper and pencil (Stage Right)

SCENE 8:
DODGER LOCKER
ROOM

Towels in all lockers
Dressing: equipment bags/comic
books/sports papers
Cigarettes/matches (Stage Left)
Rubbing Table with deck of
playing cards (Stage Right)

SCENE 9:
RICKEY'S OFFICE

Same as Scene 5, but add a contract for signing

SCENE 10:
THE PLAYING FIELD

Break-away watermelon
(Stage Left)

ACT TWO

SCENE 1:
POLO GROUNDS   1947 Dodgers' programs
                                (Stage Left)
                             Pencils (Stage Left)
                             Book with title, "The Official
                                Baseball Book of the Colored
                                Major Leagues" (Stage Left)

SCENE 2:
DODGER LOCKER   Same as Act One, Scene 8
   ROOM

SCENE 3:
BEHIND THIRD BASE
EBBETS FIELD   Three Dodgers' scorecards/pen-
                                cils (Stage Left)
                             Bag of unshelled peanuts
                                (Stage Left)

SCENE 4:
FRONT PORCH
OUTSIDE ST. LOUIS   Rocking chair
                             Straight-back chair
                             Table with phone
                             Dish Towel (Stage Right)

SCENE 5:
OUTSIDE EBBETS FIELD   Sandwich board with buttons/
                                pennants (Stage Left)
                             Cowbell inside Hilda's bag
                                (Stage Left)
                             Sandwich board with buttons/
                                pennants (Stage Right)
                             "19" and "47" cards behind
                                sandwich board (Stage Right)
                             "Brooklyn Eagle" and "Daily
                                News" (Stage Left)

SCENES 6 & 7:
INSIDE EBBETS FIELD   Bats/Balls/Gloves